TESTIMONIALS

"I applaud and appreciate Joel Goodman's pioneer-
g work on the positive power of humor. As Joel says,
Iumor is for giving!' *Laffirmations* will give you the gift
humor . . . with over 1,000 practical and playful ways
invite more humor into your life and work."

—*Steve Allen*
omedian, musician, author, creator of The Tonight Show

"A sense of humor is critical for a happy life. It can
se pain, accelerate healing, reduce tension, win friends,
hance learning and make life a fun-filled adventure.
ffirmations presents you with a thousand ways to light-
up your life. I highly recommend this book!"

—*Jack Canfield*
author, Chicken Soup for the Soul
and A 2nd Helping of Chicken Soup for the Soul

TESTIMONIALS

"Humor is a godsend that human beings need to give one another. Joel's book will lift your comic spirit. *Laffirmations* will help you add years to your life . . . and life to your years."

—Joan Borysenko, Ph.D.
author of Minding the Body, Mending the Mind
and Fire in the Soul

"If elected President of the United States, one of my first acts would be to appoint Joel Goodman as Secretary of Humor. But until that time, I would highly recommend that you buy this book!"

—Pat Paulsen
perennial presidential candidate

LAFFIRMATIONS

1,001 Ways to Add Humor to Your Life and Work

JOEL GOODMAN

With Ziggy® illustrations by Tom Wilson
© Ziggy & Friends, Inc.

Health Communications, Inc.
Deerfield Beach, Florida

Dr. Joel Goodman
Director
The HUMOR Project, Inc.
110 Spring Street
Saratoga Springs, NY 12866
(518) 587-8770

ISBN 1-55874-346-4

Published by:
Health Communications, Inc.
3201 S.W. 15th Street
Deerfield Beach, FL 33442

This book is dedicated to Adam and Alyssa.

I'm very glad that there is a May 15 and an October 14 in my life—the birthdays of my son, Adam, and my daughter, Alyssa. They are important mentors of mine 365 days a year. I love being their father . . . I love the laughter, creativity and tenderness they bring to my life. I am so thankful for the childlike perspective they rekindle in me on a daily basis.

FOREWORD

I have learned the value of healthy, child-like humor in my own life and in my work with people confronted by life-threatening situations.

Joel Goodman's *Laffirmations* will help you reset your life and see it in a new way.

Let me give you one personal example about what happens when you have humor vision. Once when driving late at night, my wife, Bobbie, decided I ought to have some coffee to keep me awake. As she poured a cupful from the thermos, the hot coffee spilled all over my lap.

Believe me, it got my attention! I said, "Thanks, hot coffee really *does* wake you up!"

Recently she spilled a hot cup of herbal tea in my lap while we were strapped in our seats on a flight. That's a lot healthier than coffee.

This book will wake you up to the positive power of healthy humor. Joel's message is about humor and laughter but it is no laughing matter. Take humor seriously. It heals relationships, diseases and keeps you young.

In short, it is physiologic to laugh. The more you talk to survivors or prisoners in bodies or buildings, you find those who are going to live through their situation have the ability to laugh at life.

I hope you can now see why Joel's book is needed.

In conclusion let me say that when I served one year as an outside advisor to the Board of Directors of Heaven, I noted something. The most frequent question asked upon arrival in Heaven was, "Why was I so serious back there?" The most frequent question on earth is, "Where's the bathroom?"

So, read on, lighten up and grow young.

—Dr. Bernie Siegel

Acknowledgments

A very special thank you to my wife, Margie. She has inspired me and conspired with me as Director of Special Programs at The HUMOR Project for the past ten years. Her feedback and support have played an important role in the evolution of this book. Her birthday is December 2—my mirthday is every day I'm with her. She's my best audience (she even appreciates my bad puns . . . if that's not redundant—is there such an animal as a good pun?). Margie is an incredibly affirming human being and humane being.

And speaking of affirming: the love and laughter from my mom and dad, brother David and sister Susan are certainly partly to blame for my off-the-beaten-career-path. My family was the inspiration for my creating The HUMOR Project in 1977.

I would like to thank The HUMOR Project staff for their behind-the-scenes help, good spirits and good work: Ellen Ciampa, Linda Coseo, Marcie DeSieno, Anita Harris, Ellen Hill, Mary Kay Rickard, Deborah Usas.

Special thanks also go to my agent, Rita Rosenkranz, for her guidance and affirmation. And finally, a big thank you to Peter Vegso and Gary Seidler of Health Communications, Inc., who have known for years that, "It's good to laugh!"

Tom Wilson is a kindred creative comic spirit. I especially appreciate his permission to include our friend, Ziggy, throughout this book. Ziggy is copyrighted by Ziggy & Friends, Inc.

There have been many other humor allies from whom I've drawn support for this book. I thank Janet Booth, Annette Craighead, Bill Dana, Tom Davis, Mary Dewar, Mary Durham, Bob Fodero, Judith Harvey, Mel Helitzer, Bob Jordan, Angela King, Karla Kizzort, Nancy Koch, Andy Kulat, Richard Lederer, Nancy Leveille, Al Mager, Mack McGinnis, Ann McGee-Cooper, Colleen McGrath, Brenda McGuire, Jeff McKay, Kyle Miller, Kenneth Newton, Laurence J. Peter, Ira Robbins, Sage Ruckterstuhl, Nancy Schmitt, V. Lynn Tyler, Glenn Van Ekeren, Fran Vincent, Carolyn Warner, Ann Weiss, Steve Wilson and Mickey Mehal Wischnewski.

I also thank my many pen pals. Each year, The HUMOR Project receives 50,000 letters from people all around the world. I appreciate the folks who contributed ideas that jump-started my brain to generate practical applications of humor.

Finally, mucho applause to the thousands of people in my programs who have come up at the end of a presentation to share a story, a funny anecdote or a practical humor tip.

WELCOME

I received a letter from a nurse who attended one of my presentations. She wrote, *I work on an obstetrical floor in a hospital. Someone recently posted an article which said, "Recent research shows that the first five minutes of life are very risky." Evidently, underneath that, someone else had pencilled in the words, "The last five minutes aren't so hot either."* Of course, in life, it's what you do in between the first five and the last five minutes that makes all the difference!

Between the front and back covers, this book aims to make a delightful difference. ***Laffirmations*** will help you to discover, recover, affirm and integrate your sense of humor in everyday life and work situations. With this timely and timeless book, you will be grinning from year to year.

This book can make a difference for you . . .

On a personal level: In a world of accelerating change, it appears that "the more things change, the more they stay insane." Lily Tomlin offers perspective on this when she says, "Even if you win the rat race, you're still a rat." People are increasingly conscious of wanting to minimize "burnout" and maximize balance in life—as reflected by the surge of interest in healthy lifestyles, wellness, spirituality, nutrition, exercise and fitness. As part of this movement, a growing number of people are starting to come to their senses . . . of humor.

On the job: A report to the President's Science Advisor places the cost of stress to the economy at $200 billion annually. Studies show that employees who have the most fun at their jobs are likely to be the most productive and that 98% of chief executives interviewed would hire a person with a good sense of humor over a straight-laced worker. Every CEO questioned praised humor as an effective way to relieve tension, build morale and bring new perspectives to serious problems. As Robin Williams says, humor is "acting out optimism."

In the midst of an all-too-serious and stress-filled world, we need to lighten up. This book moves you on a daily basis from Humor Awareness to Humor Action (H.A.H.A.)

Laffirmations contains hundreds of invitations to laugh and to affirm your sense of humor. These invitations are sprinkled throughout the book in a unique blend of:

(1) **Quotes About the Nature of Humor:** The rich compendium of quotes about humor and its kindred spirits (comedy and laughter) comes from the wit and wisdom of Bill Cosby, Lily Tomlin, Jerry Seinfield, Steve Allen, Carol Burnett, Charlie Chaplin, Bernie Siegel and others. On each page, you will find a thought-provoking, mirthful and memorable quote that will give you insight about the nature of humor and help you "make sense of humor." When the quote is from a person whose birthday occurs on that date, the person's name is preceded by a birthday cake.

(2) **Questions to Bridge the Nature and Nurture of Humor:** Each day, you'll find one or more clarifying questions that will tickle your sense of wonder (AHA) and your sense of humor (HAHA) to help you get more smileage out of life.

(3) **Prescriptions to Nurture Humor:** Drawing from my work with over 600,000 people throughout the world, these practical, life-tested tips will help you add more humor to your life and work. This goldmine of ideas includes simple, effective ways to add years to your life and life to your years.

(4) **Special Guest Appearances from Our Friend, Ziggy®:** Ziggy® gives hope and humor to the more than 100 million people who take him into their homes with the daily newspaper. This affable, laffable lover of life will visit us in this book on the first day of each month.

Actually, I have a confession to make. The subtitle, ***1001 Ways to Add Humor to Your Life and Work***, is incorrect. In fact, there are 1074 ways to enrich your life and to jump-start your sense of humor (354 days x 3 stimuli each day plus 12 Ziggy days). I thought you wouldn't mind having an extra 73 ways.

How can you get the most out of this book? Here are some user-friendly suggestions:

(1) Use the quote and question on each page as a daily meditation tool to increase your awareness of humor and to discover (and recover) the presence of humor in your life—and the presents that humor can give you. Think about the implications of the quote and question for you; then brainstorm applications for your life.

(2) This is not a "joke book." In fact, the book will help you learn hundreds of ways to invite smiles

and laughter in life without having to tell a single joke. Humor is much more than "joke-telling."

(3) Practice the tips to add more humor, joy and laughter to your life and work. Take the tips as they come, fun-day-at-a-time . . . or skip around. Today may be July 17, but you can't wait to implement the idea listed for August 5—don't defer gratification—jest do it!

(4) One size does not fit all when it comes to humor. Some of the Humor Prescriptions may not "fit" you or your situation—you be the judge. Feel free to modify or adapt these ideas to suit your personality, style and setting.

(5) Above all else, have fun! Look up your birthday or anniversary, and see if you can implement the ideas given for those days as gifts for yourself or people you care about. Whenever Ziggy® shows up in the book, have a dialogue with him. What can he teach you? How does he tickle you?

(6) Humor is for giving. And this book is for giving. Give the gift of humor to someone who needs a lift. Make every year a light year . . . a year of laughter, of affirmation, of ***Laffirmations.***

..IS LIFE REALLY JUST A GAME?...
...YES, BUT THERE IS SOME ASSEMBLY REQUIRED!
TOM WILSON

Seven days without laughter makes one weak.

—Joel Goodman

How can you make every day Funday?

In the calendar that you carry around, keep a humorous definition of stress. Whenever you're in a daze, look at your days and regain perspective. For instance, Casey Stengel, former manager of the New York Yankees, used this playful perspective: The secret of managing is to "keep the five guys who hate you away from the four . . . who are undecided."

A smile is the shortest distance between two people.

—Victor Borge

Today is Victor Borge's birthday. Can you recall a time when a smile, or laughter, brought you closer to someone else? Who can you touch today with your smile?

When things get to the point of producing anger, take on the persona of your favorite humorist and approach the situation as you think he or she would. Use the person's mannerisms, phrases, etc. If that fails, then tap dance.

Nothing is quite as funny as the unintended humor of reality.

—*Steve Allen*

When has humor in your reality surprised you?

Look for life-bloopers or unintentional humor. For instance, in a recent church bulletin, these words appeared: "The pastor will preach his farewell message, after which the choir will sing, 'Break Forth Into Joy.'"

Humor is emotional chaos remembered in tranquility.

—James Thurber

Have you ever said, "Someday, we'll laugh about this"? Why wait?

Collect newspaper headlines like, "Man Killed in Fight Over Eggs." They'll make your own hassles seem tame.

Humor is the indignification of dignity.

—Charles Chaplin

Can you remember a time in your life when the proverbial "snowball" knocked off your "top hat"? What can you do to take yourself less seriously?

Use a bogus membership card (e.g., to the ALF Fan Club) as a second means of identification after showing your driver's license. Inevitably, this gives everyone a license to laugh.

Laughter is medicine to the weary bones.

—Carl Sandburg

How can you move from "weary bones" to "funny bones"? What's one way you could give yourself a humor shot-in-the-arm this week?

When dealing with aging, lighten the load by using the expression, "There is nothing wrong with getting old as long as you keep on doing it. It's when you stop doing it that your troubles really start."

True humor is a sort of train wreck of the mind. You're going along a track and there's a sudden collapse of logic, the cars go off the track, and then they pile up and build into laughter.

—Norman Cousins

Can you recall a time when logic got you into a heap of trouble? How can you use laughter to derail your thinking and increase your creativity?

When people say, "Have a nice day," simply respond, "Thanks, but I have other plans." They'll listen . . . and laugh.

Laughter is the natural sound of childhood.

—*Alvin Schwartz*

Can you remember how you laughed as a child? How about returning to those thrilling days of yesteryear . . . by trying out your childhood laugh?

Use kids' birthday toys at your adult dinner parties to bring out the playful child in everyone!

Humor puts things in perspective and helps us to see things inside out and upside down. Humor requires thought and a strong degree of compassion.

—Jerry and Helen Weiss

What do you feel passionate and compassionate about? How can you inject humor into your passion and compassion?

When confronting your fears, remember this story: There was a storm one night, and a little boy was afraid. He woke up and came into his parents' bedroom saying, "Daddy, I'm scared." The father reassured him, "Don't worry, son, God loves you." The boy replied, "I know, Daddy, but right now I need someone with skin on."

Nonsense is probably the greatest discipline of all. Word play is as disciplined an enterprise as you can undertake.

—*Willard Espy*

What was your favorite riddle as a kid? How does it relate to an "adult riddle" you are trying to figure out in your own life now?

Play with the meaning, sound and look of words by creating sentences such as this: "You can lead a horse to water, but a pencil must be lead."

Humor results when society says you can't scratch certain things in public, but they itch in public.

—*Father Tom Walsh*

So, how do you handle embarrassment?

Take yourself less seriously. Put your degrees (BA, PhD, RN, MSW) on your bathroom wall. When people visit and ask why they are there, simply say, "This is 'the library' in our house!"

Wrinkles should merely indicate where the smiles have been.

—Mark Twain

What are three places in your life that bring out a smile in you? What about these places tickles you so?

To develop your comic vision, look for examples of humor and irony in the environment—then photograph them.

Laughter is not at all a bad beginning for a friendship, and it is by far the best ending for one.

—*Oscar Wilde*

Which friends tickle your funnybone the most? How do they do it? Whose funnybone do you tickle?

Throw yourself a surprise party. You invite people, and they bring their surprises.

Humor is laughing at what you haven't got when you ought to have it.

—Langston Hughes

What's missing in your life now? What's funny about it?

When in doubt, revert to humor. Whenever anything unbelievable happens to you, just say, "It's only a movie!"

Anyone who has had the job I've had and didn't have a sense of humor wouldn't still be here.

—Harry Truman

What's the most challenging part of your job? How can you inject humor into that part of your job?

In your office, have a brown paper grocery bag with eye-holes cut in it. If anyone pulls a blooper and is feeling somewhere between "embarrassed" and "mortified," he or she simply dons the bag, which invites everyone to laugh together. One man tells us, "The other day, I was using the toilet, and when I stood up, my pager fell off my belt. It not only plugged the toilet, but we could not retrieve it (not that we wanted to) . . . and we had to get a new toilet. I could have worn the bag myself for about a month—I certainly was flushed with embarrassment!"

Humor is a wonderful way to prevent a hardening of the attitudes!

—Joel Goodman

What can you do today to stay flexible in body, mind and spirit?

Hold dress-up parties at the wrong times—for instance, beach parties in the winter. In humor, as you know, (wrong) timing is everything!

We rarely succeed at anything unless we have fun doing it.

—Rev. John Naus

What are three successes you've had in life? How have they brought you joy?

Collect pictures of famous people and autograph them yourself with "personal" messages. Hang them up on the wall. You'll have fun with people who come into your office.

Humor is music to the soul, and you don't have to carry a tune—just sing along!

—John Richardson

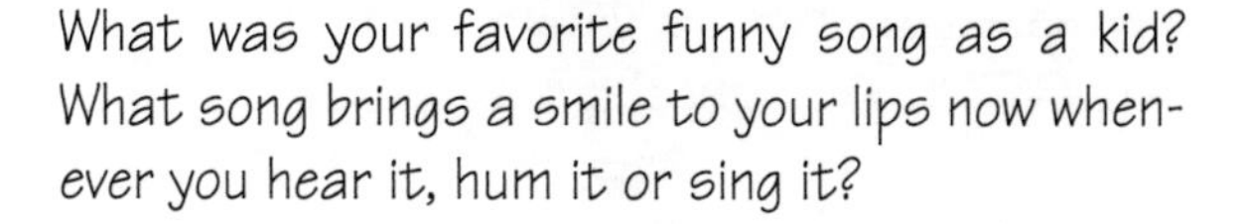

What was your favorite funny song as a kid? What song brings a smile to your lips now whenever you hear it, hum it or sing it?

When your spouse gets too serious on a subject, break out in "Row, row, row your boat"—it can be a byword for you both to lighten up.

I don't make jokes. I just watch the government and report the facts.

—Will Rogers

In celebration of Inauguration Day, what about our government do you find laughable? What would Will Rogers say about it today?

When things get hot and heavy in your organization, make up outrageous ideas for fund-raising—like having a seed-spitting contest between the mayor and city manager.

It is bad to suppress laughter. It goes back down and spreads to your hips.

—Fred Allen

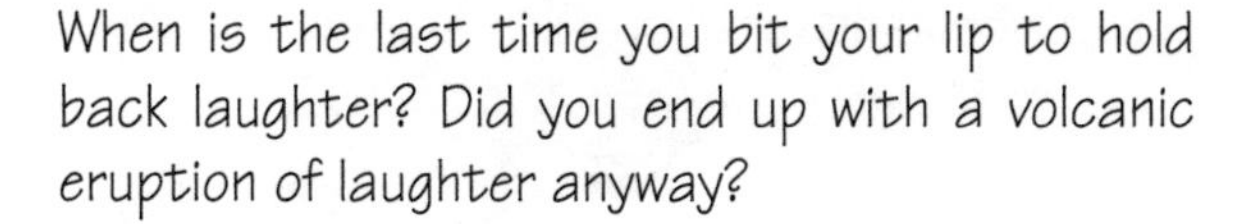

When is the last time you bit your lip to hold back laughter? Did you end up with a volcanic eruption of laughter anyway?

Inject humor into an otherwise-tense situation. Place some cartoons in a stack of work that a coworker is tackling, in a test that students are taking, on the breakfast tray of someone in the hospital.

Humor is the ability to see three sides of one coin.

—Ned Rorem

In a challenge you are facing now, what is the "third right answer"?

When a situation is out of hand at the office, get your hands on juggling blocks labeled "Yes," "No" and "Forget It." The first one to fall doesn't really make the call, but it is a tension-breaker.

Laugh at yourself first, before anyone else can.

—Elsa Maxwell

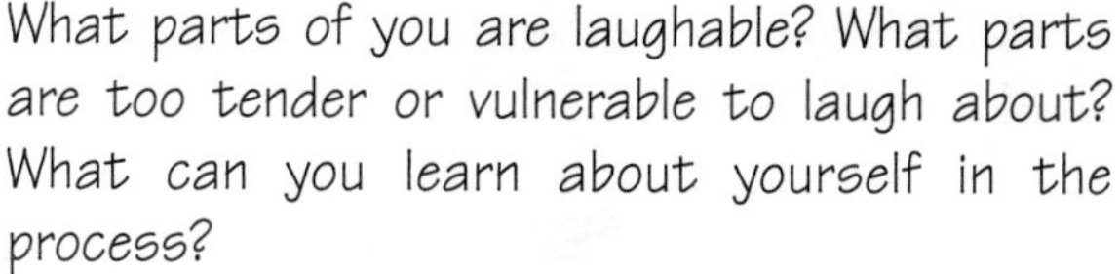

What parts of you are laughable? What parts are too tender or vulnerable to laugh about? What can you learn about yourself in the process?

Collect humorous incidents that you observe in everyday life. A teacher passed along this example: Her first-grade students were going through the lunch line. A little girl asked for "pisketti." A boy laughed at the pronunciation. Another girl said, "Don't make fun of her. She has an accident from New Jersey."

Humor turns us on mentally and activates both brain hemispheres.

—William Fry, Jr., M.D.

What turns you on in life? When do you feel most alive?

Cut funny pictures out of magazines. At parties or family gatherings, have your friends and family make up captions for these pictures.

Caricature is putting the face of a joke upon the body of a truth.

—Joseph Conrad

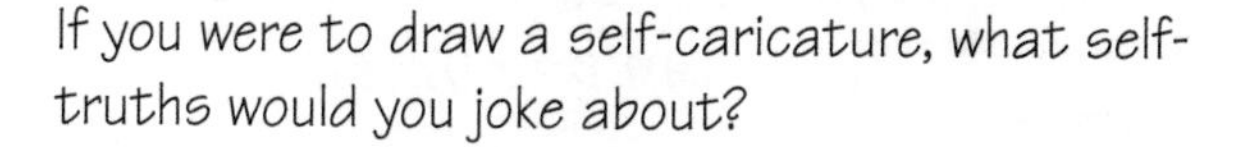

If you were to draw a self-caricature, what self-truths would you joke about?

In your family, set yourself up so your kids can see you laughing at yourself for "failing." Model that it's okay to grow up and not be perfect. For a week, let the kids mark the calendar with a playful sticker when Mom or Dad are wrong or do something silly. This will help all of you laugh with one another when you're not perfect.

You've got to laugh at yourself sometimes. If you can't climb the mountain of yourself head-on, you've got to find a flight of stairs that no one has discovered before. Those stairs can be humor.

—*Jules Feiffer*

In celebrating Jules Feiffer's birthday, ask yourself: "What important goals do I have that humor could help me achieve?"

Remember the saying, "Life is what happens when you're making other plans." It will help you to see humor in everyday life.

Laugh while you can. There is nothing more biodegradable than happiness.

—Mary Durham

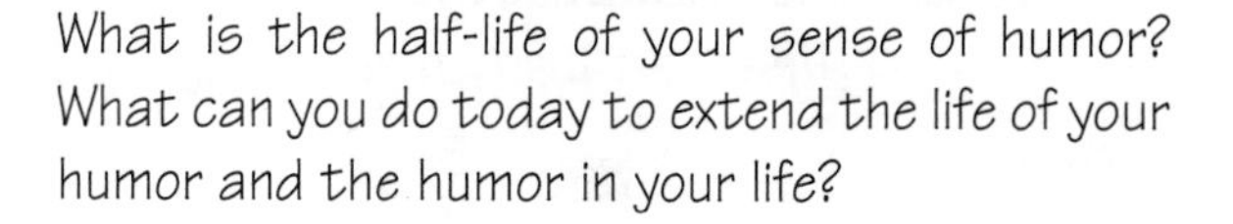

What is the half-life of your sense of humor? What can you do today to extend the life of your humor and the humor in your life?

Make all your own greeting cards by saving any cartoons, quotes or images that might be a reminder of a funny incident involving the person receiving the card. For example, one man got a cartoon about a bigger, better "fly eliminator" on his Christmas card, because the previous summer he had broken a window playing Great Hunter with a fly swatter.

We had a seriousness of purpose. We also believed the old saying that to be serious doesn't mean to be solemn. We reveled in our lack of solemnity.

*—Alan Alda*

Today is M*A*S*H star Alan Alda's birthday. Where do you draw the line between "being serious" and "being solemn"?

Make a deliberate effort to provide "laugh time" for yourself on a daily basis. Try watching television programs like M*A*S*H *or* Mary Tyler Moore *re-runs to release tension.*

That is the best—to laugh with someone because you both think the same things are funny.

—Gloria Vanderbilt

What common sense(s) of humor do you share with three of your closest friends?

Keep a humor scrapbook with your spouse of all the funny cartoons and anecdotes you find that remind you of each other and your home life. Review and chuckle over them every year on your anniversary—we who laugh last . . .

You don't have to teach people to be funny. You only have to give them permission.

—Harvey Mindess

What will it take to give yourself permission to be funny?

Give yourself license to use humor by ordering a customized license plate—e.g., OK TO WAVE, Y RESIST.

If you could choose one characteristic that would get you through life, choose a sense of humor.

—Jennifer James

When and how did humor help you make it through a crunch time in your life?

When in the midst of an anxiety-producing moment, stop, take a step back and say, "This could be amusing." It will remind you to see the humor in each situation.

THINGS TO DO TODAY
1. inhale
2. exhale
3. inhale
4. exhale
5. inhale
6. exhale
7. inhale
8. exhale
9. inhale
10. exhale
11. inhale
12. exhale
13. inhale

Just say YO!

—Tommy Smothers

What would you like to say YO! to in your life?

Celebrate Tommy's birthday by buying (or dusting off) a yo-yo. Take some time to play with it . . . and to laugh at yourself in the process as you "learn the ropes."

There are three rules for creating humor, but unfortunately no one knows what they are.

—Laurence J. Peter

If you could make up three rules for creating humor, what would they be?

Catch yourself having fun three times today.

You only get good by bombing.

—*David Brenner*

When in your life have you bombed? What did you learn from that experience? How is your risk-taking quotient today?

Go to a local comedy club. For extra credit, take the risk of performing stand-up at open mike night.

Humor is a reaffirmation of life.

—Bea Berry

What is important to you today? How can you reaffirm this in your actions?

Spend more time with people who make you laugh. Seek the positive contagion of laughter. Let go of seeing things too seriously. Acknowledge the absurd and roll with the inconsistencies of life.

A good laugh is sunshine in a house.

—William Thackeray

How can you add more humor to your ho-ho-home?

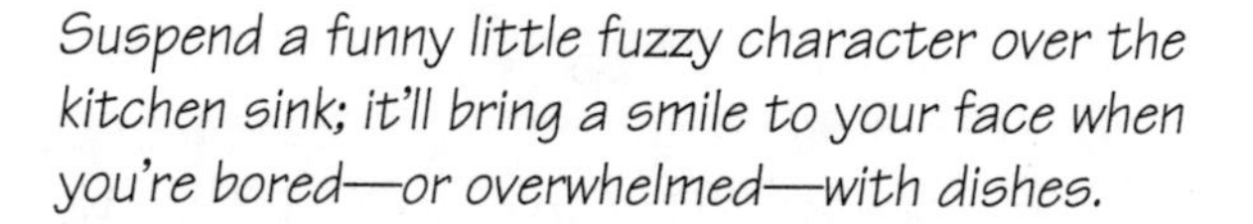

Suspend a funny little fuzzy character over the kitchen sink; it'll bring a smile to your face when you're bored—or overwhelmed—with dishes.

This is what it's all about: If you can't have fun at it, there's no sense hanging around.

—*Joe Montana*

What part of your life isn't fun right now? How can you add some humor to it?

Put up a poster behind your desk that tickles your funnybone. For instance, "Eat a small toad in the morning, and it will be the worse thing you do all day."

Comedy is a mysterious and unexplored art.

—*Robert Klein*

What would you use to explore humor: a telescope, a microscope or a kaleidoscope? What would you discover?

Hang a sign in your office: "Life's too mysterious . . . don't take it too serious!"

Humor is the prelude to faith and laughter is the beginning of prayer.

—Reinhold Niebuhr

How do you keep the faith, keep perspective and keep on truckin' in your life?

Places of worship can be serious places. And yet, humor resides there! Every time you go, make a point to look for laughter. For example, there was a sign at a church that read, "Baked Bean Supper—Band Concert to Follow." What a gas!

Humor and creativity are intimately related—there is a connection between HAHA and AHA.

—Joel Goodman

What's one thing you've done lately that was creative?

Pretend that difficult situations are not real, but rather scenes from a play by Neil Simon. Then "play" with the difficulty.

Laugh and the world laughs with you. Cry and you may not cry alone, but you'll get a group discount.

—Etruscan Philosopher

Who is a supportive person for you? Whose laugh is contagious for you? When did you last spend time with these people?

Get a gang together. The more the merrier. You can often get a group discount if you round up ten or more people—go to a dinner theater to see a comedy, go to a sporting event, go to a comedy club, whatever!

My mission is through laughter to bring people together—to be the Martin Luther King of comedy.

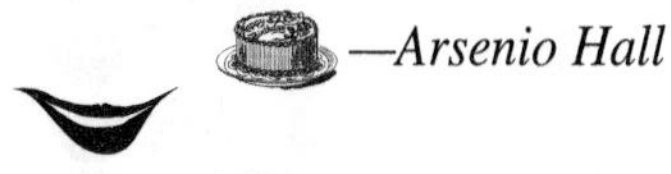

—*Arsenio Hall*

Can you recall a time that humor helped to bring a group together?

Interject humor at meetings charged with emotion. For instance, when there is an interpersonal conflict in a meeting, the people involved are charged to bring in a humorous cartoon or joke to the next meeting. Humor can be a way for folks to move from a "life-or-death, you-are-the-enemy" mentality to a "we're-in-this-boat-together" orientation.

February 13

In life, pain is inevitable, but suffering is optional.

—Hedy Schleifer

How can you use humor today to alleviate suffering?

Charity (and humor) may indeed begin at home. Auction off a joke-a-day (from you for a year) for a charitable cause. Enlist all your friends to dig up jokes for you to use in this venture.

Love may make the world go round, but laughter keeps us from getting dizzy.

—Donald Zochert

How do you keep your balance in life?

Try to lighten up the dating scene with the following self-talk: "It's good to marry. By all means do it. If you get a good spouse, you'll be happy. If you get a bad one, you'll be a philosopher."

To make mistakes is human; to stumble is commonplace; to be able to laugh at yourself is maturity.

—*William Arthur Ward*

Are you making enough mistakes?

Keep track of your faux pas. For example, on one occasion a woman and her husband were traveling in Germany. They stopped in what she thought was a clothing store. It turned out to be a dry cleaner's. She was trying on other people's laundry. The dry cleaner is probably still shaking his head and laughing.

A good laugh is a mighty good thing and rather too scarce a good thing.

—*Herman Melville*

Have you achieved your minimum daily requirement of 15 laughs today?

Write fake prescriptions for other people (and for yourself). For example, "Take laughter 4 times daily—Signed, Y.B. Grumpy, M.D." or "One hour quiet time daily—Signed, R.E. Lax, M.D."

One thing I've learned about humor is that it's never quite so funny as when your situation is almost hopeless. You're dealing with an absurdity, and the humor arises out of the absurdity.

—Pat McManus

Where is the humor in an absurd, hopeless, seemingly humorless situation you're now facing?

Use the humor skill of reversal. Whenever you're having a bad day, stop completely whatever you're doing and pause for a moment. Reflect on things that make you happy and reasons you could be smiling. It's amazing how quickly this can turn your mood around.

If you lose your power to laugh, you lose your power to think.

—Diane Benton, first grade teacher of Adam Goodman

What do you think about the quote above?

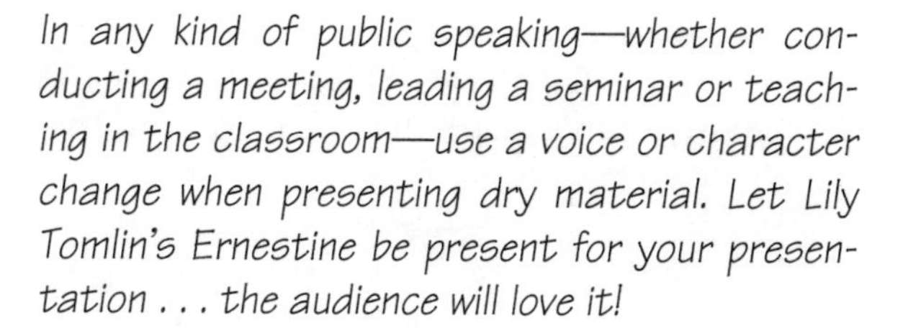

In any kind of public speaking—whether conducting a meeting, leading a seminar or teaching in the classroom—use a voice or character change when presenting dry material. Let Lily Tomlin's Ernestine be present for your presentation . . . the audience will love it!

Most folks are about as happy as they make up their minds to be.

—Abraham Lincoln

How happy do you make up your mind to be?

When things are tough at work, ask each other, "Are we having fun yet?" Then take a "happy minute" (as opposed to a "happy hour") to get a humorous perspective on the situation.

Humorists are serious. They are the only people who are.

—Mark Van Doren

What's one thing about which you are serious? Any thoughts on how to lighten it up?

On family automobile trips, you and your kids can don Groucho glasses. Watch the reaction of other motorists. It helps "break up" the trip.

When humor goes, there goes civilization.

—*Erma Bombeck*

Can you recall a time when humor helped you remain civilized?

The next time you are part of an insane situation, step back mentally and ask yourself how Erma Bombeck would describe the situation in her column. When you distance yourself from stress in this way, you can laugh at the absurdity of it.

People who laugh at death feel superior to those who are dead.

—Fred Allen

How has humor helped you in a life-or-death situation?

Always look for humor in the check-out line at the grocery store. You'll find gems like this on the news rack: A magazine cover story, "God Is Dead!" Next to it, a tabloid with the headline, "Elvis Is Alive!"

Where humor is concerned, there are no standards—no one can say what is good or bad, although you can be sure that everyone will.

—John Kenneth Galbraith

Where and how do you draw the line between "clean humor" and "dirty humor"?

Have your coworkers bring in pictures of themselves as babies in diapers. Put these (nameless) photos up on a bulletin board as a playful reminder to keep the humor "clean."

If you are going to tell people the truth, you'd better make them laugh. Otherwise they'll kill you.

—George Bernard Shaw

Can you recall a time that you, as messenger, were "killed"? How could you have injected humor to help deliver the message?

Add humorous notes or cartoons to invoices as a way of combining money and funny. Who knows, you may even help people look forward to getting their bills.

A good laugh is like manure to a farmer—it doesn't do any good until you spread it around.

—Michael Pritchard

What can you do today to spread some good cheer?

When a friend has a bad day, blow up a balloon, tape a humorous card to it, and then tape them both to the person's front door that evening—so it is there when he or she gets up in the morning.

Does God have a sense of humor? He must have if He made us.

—*Jackie Gleason*

What is the connection between your comic spirit and your spirituality?

Every night, write a diary of funny things your children do and say. Someday, give these diaries to your children as gifts. One man gave an example from his five-year-old daughter. His daughter was asked if she knew what a hearse was. She replied, "I don't know what it's called, but I know you have to be real sick to hide in it!"

Trying to define humor is one of the definitions of humor.

—*Saul Steinberg*

Charles M. Schulz wrote *Happiness Is A Warm Puppy*, a book featuring Snoopy. If you were to come up with a metaphorical book title, *Humor Is* ___ how would you playfully fill-in the blank?

Create your own acronyms for "HUMOR" and "LAUGHTER"; for example, one patient at Sunnyview Hospital said that LAUGHTER stands for "Love And Understanding Give Hope Toward Emotional Recovery."

If you don't learn to laugh at trouble, you won't have anything to laugh at when you grow old.

—Ed Howe

What is a trouble you can look forward to laughing at when you grow old?

At work, when confronted by an impossible or bizarre situation, simply start humming the theme song from The Twilight Zone.

Smile—it's lighter than you think!

—Joel Goodman

Have you noticed that you feel better when you smile?

To encourage good customer service (and positive customers), put this sign up in your workplace: "Our Return Policy: All Smiles Will Be Returned!"

WORRYIN' IS LIKE ROCKIN' IN A ROCKIN' CHAIR ...IT GIVES YOU SOMETHING TO DO...BUT IT DOESN'T GET YOU ANYWHERE
TOM WILSON

From there to here, from here to there, funny things are everywhere.

—*Dr. Seuss*

What are three funny things you've seen or heard today?

Keep a "Lipley's Believe It or Not" scrapbook of funny things that leap out of your grandchildren's lips. One grandma passed on the following true tale: Two of her friends were visiting. One wanted a glass of water. Her four-year-old granddaughter brought it to her. When the second guest asked for some water, the granddaughter said, "I can't get it—my brother's sitting on the toilet now." At that point, the first friend started gagging . . . and everyone started giggling.

You grow up the day you have your first real laugh—at yourself.

—Ethel Barrymore

When did you have your first good laugh at yourself?

Make a sign to remind you to laugh at yourself: "I am a classic underachiever. No matter how low I set my goals, I can always manage to slide in under them."

If you've got something funny to do, you don't have to be funny doing it.

—Charlie Chaplin

What's something funny you can do today?

Look for the ridiculous and far-out in everyday life. Keep your ears and eyes open in public places. Make crazy gifts—like mittens with "right" and "left" embroidered on the wrong hands.

Humor is the catharsis through which a society purges its demons.

—*Clifton Jolley*

Have you had your laughter catharsis today?

Compile a comedic communication book for different shifts or departments in your organization. Always try to bring in a "thought for the day" to write in the book. An example from Mae West: "When given a choice of two evils, I always take the one I never tried before."

Humor arises directly from the process of perception which allows the mind to switch over and look at something in a completely new way.

—Edward de Bono

What is something new that you notice about an old familiar object (like your watch or a dollar bill)?

Celebrate Lou Costello's birthday. Use tapes of comedy routines, like Abbott and Costello's Who's on First?, *to help you switch over your mind.*

We should be proud of who we are. Then we can laugh at ourselves. Being natural, being yourself goes right to the heart of humor.

—Willard Scott

What do you feel proud about in your life? What brings a smile to you when you think of your accomplishments?

In order to keep your sanity, collect humorous triumphs of the human spirit. For example, a flight attendant was bending over to give a passenger a drink when a male passenger behind her (slightly drunk) put his hand on her fanny. Without skipping a beat, she turned to him, smiled sweetly and said, "I'm sorry, sir. You didn't pay for that seat!"

Everything is funny as long as it is happening to someone else.

—Will Rogers

Can you think of someone to whom "it" has happened recently? How could you reach out and touch them with humor?

Buy funny greeting cards. Keep them . . . until the time is right. When you have friends, relatives or co-workers who would appreciate particular cards, send them.

There's no time like the pleasant.

—Oliver Herford

When you are present, you can experience the pleasant. How do you get yourself in the here-and-now?

Collect the gems from the mouths of young people. Recently, for instance, a second grader went to the school secretary and said that his teacher wanted some "gin tape." The secretary said, "Do you mean masking tape?" The boy, "No, gin tape." The secretary called the teacher via the intercom and asked what she wanted. It turns out that she wanted Scotch™ tape. Another kid was overheard while playing with dolls, "Do you take this man to be your awfully wedded husband?"

Humor affirms our humanity.

—*Milton Friedman*

What is most human about you? What is most humorous about you? Are the two connected?

When your office is in the midst of a crisis, keep perspective by using humorous quotes like, "There is no such thing as failure—only successes we don't like very much."

Humor is a means by which people try to order and make sense of what they're doing.

—Joseph Boskin

What in your life is in order? What is out of order? How can humor be of help to you in either arena?

There seem to be at least two kinds of people in the world: the "desk messies" and the "desk neatniks." Put a sign on the top of your piles: "Don't clear up my desk—you'll mess up my system!"

A *good* laugh is the best pesticide.

—Vladimir Nabokov

What is it that bugs you? How can you use humor with your "pest peeves"?

When in the middle (or muddle) of a stressful situation, imagine how you would see this situation 20 years from now. Then you'll really see the humor in it.

Our job is to make audiences laugh and feel good, and the only way to do that is to be real...You don't look for the laugh. You play it for reality first, and then you can add on the jokes.

—Bill Cosby

How can you be "real" today? How can you be true to yourself and laugh at your reality at the same time?

When frustrated with obstinate teenage demands, simply think to yourself, "How can I take seriously anyone who acts like that?" (Of course, your teenager may use the same strategy.)

Humor is the healthy way of feeling a "distance" between one's self and the problem, a way of standing off and looking at one's problem with perspective.

—Rollo May

What's a problem that's been staring you in the face lately? How does it look from 20 paces?

When everyone at the office is stressed out, just use the expression, "It's not brain surgery." This may help you to cut through the tension.

Jesters do often prove prophets.

—William Shakespeare—celebrate the Ides of March!

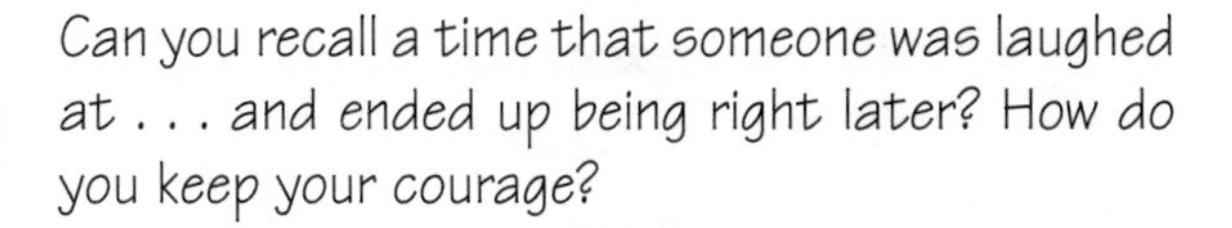

Can you recall a time that someone was laughed at . . . and ended up being right later? How do you keep your courage?

Think of a common machine or appliance you use in your home or office. Have some fun by developing a Rube Goldberg-like invention to perform the same function in a much more complicated way.

In friendship let there be laughter and sharing of pleasures.

—Kahlil Gibran

What flavors of humor do you enjoy sharing with your friends?

If people you love are far away, send them a Care Package each week filled with funny clippings. They can draw from the package whenever they feel lonely or low. This is a great way to "reach out and touch someone" across the miles (and the smiles).

Humor is one way of creating people who are inverse paranoids—people who think the world is out to do them good.

—Joel Goodman

Today's your lucky day. What's one thing you can do to help other people think the world is out to do them good?

Put different humorous posters around the office at stressful times, and never in the same place. When the humor is on-the-wall, it helps us when we're off-the-wall.

A comedian says funny things.
A comic says things funny.

—*Michael Davis*

Can you recall a time you put your foot in your mouth? What funny thing do you have to say about it now?

Take on the challenge of saying a tongue twister five times during the course of the day. Peter Piper picked a peck of tickled peppers . . .

Work consists of whatever a body is obliged to do. Play consists of whatever a body is not obliged to do.

—Mark Twain

How do you balance work and play in your life? Or do you?

Get playful props for your home or office; a Kermit the Frog telephone can keep you from croaking in the midst of challenging conversations.

Laughing is a great release. So is crying. It's important to realize there's more to comedy than laugh tracks and off-color humor.

—Sid Caesar

Have you ever laughed so hard you cried? Have you ever been crying hard and then found yourself laughing?

Think of a humorous ritual you can create when your extended family gets together. One man told us that when his family got together for holidays at his grandparents' home, the big question each year was, "Can Uncle Leonard make Grandma laugh hard enough to wet her pants?" The laughter really flowed!

If you haven't got a sense of humor, you haven't got any sense at all.

—Mary McDonald

If you ever misplaced your sense of humor, where would you look for it?

Make up a sign for your desk that says, "I don't remember what I wanted to be when I grew up . . . but I'm sure it wasn't this." This is especially helpful when you lose sight of what you're doing and why you're doing it.

Most of the time I don't have much fun. The rest of the time I don't have any fun at all.

—*Woody Allen*

Today is National Goof-Off Day. What can you not do to celebrate it?

In your meetings, go for the jocular vein, not the jugular vein. Wear camouflage helmets to your next meeting as a light-hearted way to make a point: meetings need not be deadly serious.

Progress is nothing but the victory of laughter over dogma.

—Benjamin DeCasseres

Do you ever say, "But we've always done it this way"? If so, how could you do it differently?

Pre-arrange some ridiculous routines. For instance, at home, whenever there is a loud and large disagreement, someone can yell "FIRE!" You must then run around the outside of the house once. This inevitably will lead to laughter and cooling off.

Laugh and the world laughs with you. Snore and you sleep alone.

—Anthony Burgess

Can you recall any funny dreams you've had? What do they tell you about yourself?

In your imagination, visualize your associates reliving serious situations dressed as clowns.

And what about this piece of advice: "Let a smile be your umbrella." I tried that once. I had pneumonia for six weeks and shrunk a $450 suit.

—George Burns

What advice would you give someone who wanted to develop his or her sense of humor?

Start a humorous tee shirt collection. Just like athletes at international soccer matches, exchange fun tee shirts with others. Wear these tee shirts to exercise your sense of humor when you are exercising—like the man who always goes jogging in his "Catatonic State" tee shirt.

Forgive, O Lord, my little jokes on Thee
And I'll forgive Thy great big one on me.

—*Robert Frost*

Who or what do you need to forgive? How can humor be an ally in accomplishing this?

Find signs that deliver serious messages with a light touch. One vet, for instance, has a doggone funny sign on the side of his clinic: "Parking for veterinary clients only. Violators will be neutered!"

The pun is the lowest form of humor—it is the basic building block.

—*Mike Thaler*

What do you think is the basic building block of humor? Can you play with this block?

Be playful and punful. Cut the zipper off an old pair of pants, bring it to work and put it in your soup at lunch when no one is looking. Then pull it out with your spoon and yell in horror and amazement, "Look! There's a fly in my soup!"

There is a dearth of mirth on the earth.

—*Bill Nelson*

What can you do to increase the mirth rate?

Set up a TGIF joke network. At 4:45 p.m. on any Friday, one person calls another with a joke. In turn, that person calls another person. The intent: to leave work at the end of the week with a smile.

The best doctors in the world are Doctor Diet, Doctor Quiet and Doctor Merryman.

—*Jonathan Swift*

What prescription would you write yourself to add more humor to your life today?

If you're on a strict diet (again), post signs on the refrigerator, like "No gain, no pain!" and "If you wanna be thinner, go easy on dinner!"

What makes something funny is a new insight into a shared experience.

—*James McConnell*

What is an insight you've shared with a friend?

Make or buy a plaque that has a very harried-looking person on it who says, "Leave me alone—I'm having a CRISIS!" Pass it around from person to person when someone is having a bad time and put your names on the back. It can help everyone realize that we all have challenges.

God purposely created fools to minister to the wise.

—*J. Olowo Ojoade*

What's something positively foolish you can do tomorrow?

Get revenge on voice mail. Surprise one another at work by putting joke phone messages into each other's mailboxes, like a phone message to call a certain number and ask for Mr. Dolphin at the local aquarium.

MIGHTY FUNNY WEATHER LATELY!

**Remember—laughing matters—
it really does!**

—Joel Goodman

What can you do to remind yourself of the importance of humor—especially when the going gets rough?

In setting agendas for potentially boring meetings, list each agenda item as a familiar song title. Of chorus, it's fun to see if participants can "name that tune" and identify the agenda items to be discussed.

Comedy is talking about things that people think about . . . and that you have in common with someone else.

—*Eddie Murphy*

What's been on your mind lately? Have your brainwaves been in synch with anyone else's?

Make magazine-cut-out-books for family and friends. Tailor-make the humor in them for each person and his or her life experiences. These books will be in great demand—it's a fun way to connect with people you care about.

People crave laughter as if it were an essential amino acid.

—Patch Adams

How do you satisfy your comedic cravings?

Buy humorous stickers or buttons and then have them handy to give out spontaneously. They always bring a smile.

The freedom of any society varies proportionately with the volume of its laughter.

—Zero Mostel

What frees up the laughter in you?

Whenever you start to lose perspective and your sense of humor, just say to yourself, "I won't know the difference 100 years from now."

A clown is a poet in action.

—*Henry Miller*

How do you clown around?

Be a card-carrying humorist. Have a business card which has the following printed on both sides: "How to drive yourself crazy (over)."

I enjoy a good laugh—one that rushes out of one's soul like the breaking up of a Sunday School.

—Josh Billings

What is the soul of humor for you?

Invite your kids, or the child in you, to see the silly side of things. Think of what a five-year-old would like to do. Have a squirt gun fight or eat pudding with your fingers. It's a good way to connect with the kid in you.

There is no cure for birth or death save to enjoy the interval.

—George Santayana

What are 20 things that you enjoy doing? How many of them have you done recently?

Give yourself a homework assignment to do at least one fun thing for yourself daily. Then have a "fun show-and-tell" with your friends, family or coworkers. This could help expand everyone's repertoire of ways to be good and fun to ourselves.

Start every day with a smile and get it over with.

—*W.C. Fields*

What's one way you could start every day with a smile? How about a way to end every day with a smile?

Keep a joke-of-the-day posted at the time clock at work. At the beginning of the day, form a "punch-line" and start the day with a smile.

The job of satire is to frighten and enlighten.

—Richard Condon

What scares you? What en-lightens your mental load? Can you put the two together?

To help car trips go faster, be on the lookout for funny signs—like the one on a back road leading to the Forest Lawn Cemetery: "Don't Honk—No One Will Answer!"

Wit is the clash and reconcilement of incongruities, the meeting of extremes around a corner.

—Leigh Hunt

What is one of your on-going life paradoxes or dilemmas? How can humor help you reconcile this internal conflict?

Look for the inadvertent juxtapositions in life—like the sign in front of a Salvation Army office that said, "Jesus Saves. Hours 9-5 Monday-Friday."

A humorist is a person who feels bad but who feels good about it.

—Don Herold

How can you use humor to move from feeling bad to feeling good today?

Celebrate David Letterman's birthday by watching Dave's monologue on your VCR this morning before going to work. Share the jokes you hear with others.

Humor is the natural response to a sudden shift in frames . . . The physiological result is a delightful symphony of good feelings.

—Joan Borysenko

What are the good feelings that humor invites in you?

Happy birthday, Thomas Jefferson! Agree with Tom's notion: "I have nothing but contempt for the person who can only find one way to spell a word." Keep a "spell-checkered" list of spelling slips—like the church blooper passed on to us: "The choir will now sin in unison."

I would like to help people smile . . . Real revolutionaries are people who look with a deep sense of humor upon their institutions.

—Ivan Illich

What's so funny about your organization?

If you work in a business where there are a lot of I-told-you-so's, develop a buzz phrase to help you laugh your way through the Monday-morning quarterbacking: "REMEMBER: Whenever something goes wrong, there's always somebody who knew it would."

The monuments of wit survive the monuments of power.

—Francis Bacon

On this most taxing of days, how can you use humor to survive?

With your staff, create a "pity pot" to help on those days when "nobody knows the troubles I've seen." Just jot a little note on whatever might be bugging you, toss it in the pot, laugh, and keep on going.

Life is a tragedy when seen in close-up, but a comedy in longshot.

—*Charlie Chaplin*

How can you keep humor up-close in your personal life?

Keep short, sweet quotes in your wallet, like "Enjoy life—this is not a dress rehearsal." When you are out-of-kilter, pull out the quotes and regain your balance.

People are more fun than anybody.

—Dorothy Parker

What do you enjoy doing most with others?

Clip cartoons appropriate to family interests and put them on each person's placemat before dinner. Starting the meal with a laugh helps you to connect after being apart during the day, and helps you to digest (the day and the food).

Being "funny" doesn't mean you aren't serious. Too many people are going around with their chins on their chests.

—Gene Shalit

How do you balance being "serious" and "funny"? Can you have both in your life and work?

As a way of not taking yourself too seriously, use your computer printer to make a poster that says, "I thought I made a mistake once . . . but I was mistaken."

Despair affects the immune system . . . I try to leave patients with something to smile about.

—Bernie Siegel

What can you do today to leave others smiling?

Put a card in your spouse's lunch along with an EKG strip under which you write, "My heart beats for you." It will bring out a hearty laugh.

Be eccentric—it's one of the few places left that's not crowded.

—Luke Barber

How does it feel to be eccentric? What would help you to move out of your "comfort zone" toward "eccentric"?

If you are facing deadlines at work and don't want to be interrupted, post a sign on your door that reads, "Don't disturb me—I'm disturbed enough already!"

The best comedy comes from children.

—Hal Roach

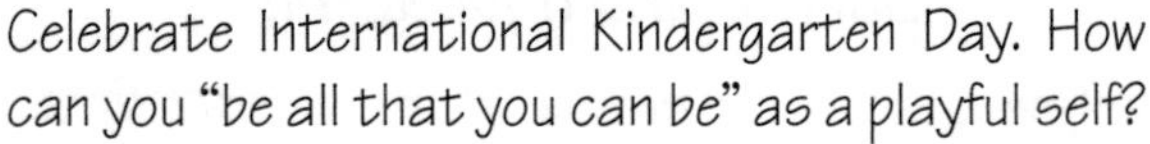

Celebrate International Kindergarten Day. How can you "be all that you can be" as a playful self?

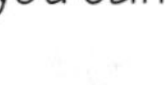

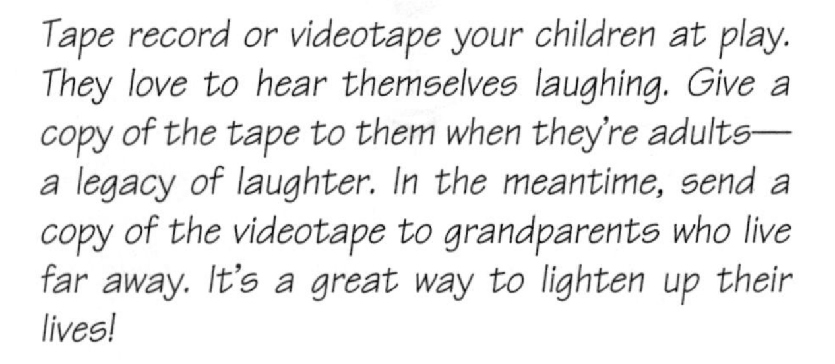

Tape record or videotape your children at play. They love to hear themselves laughing. Give a copy of the tape to them when they're adults—a legacy of laughter. In the meantime, send a copy of the videotape to grandparents who live far away. It's a great way to lighten up their lives!

A good sense of humor helps us in many ways. It helps us understand the orthodox, tolerate the unpleasant, overcome the unexpected, and survive the unbearable.

—*Gene Brown*

How has humor helped you to do any or all of the above?

Whenever the stuff is hitting the fan, you and your coworkers can try to make up a situation that would be even worse than the one you're in. Have fun with the "It Could Be Worse . . ." game.

According to the book *American Averages*, Americans laugh an average of 15 times a day. Just think, by increasing your laugh quotient, you can add light years to your life.

—Joel Goodman

Celebrate Reading Is Fun Week: Who is your favorite humorous writer?

Whenever you go to a conference or on a trip, get lost in the humor section of a local bookstore. Look for books to bring back to your friends, family or yourself! It's fun thinking about what will bring a smile to their faces—and your own face!

Laughter removes the burden of seriousness from the problem, and oftentimes, it's that very serious attitude that is the problem itself.

—*Bob Basso*

What can you do today to turn a problem into a challenge into an opportunity?

When an issue is getting too serious, pull out the tongue-in-cheek quote, "I may not always be right, but I'm never in doubt."

Humor is something that causes a tickling of the brain. Laughter is invented to scratch it.

—Hugh Foot

What has tickled your curiosity lately? What has tickled your funnybone? How might the two be related?

Find ways to tickle technology. For instance, when blow dryers replaced paper towels in the men's rest room at work, there were many instructions for their use posted on the bathroom wall. At the end, someone had written, "Wipe your hands on your pants."

Comedy is tragedy plus time.

—Carol Burnett

What is something you face now that appears to be tragic but in ten years will be comic?

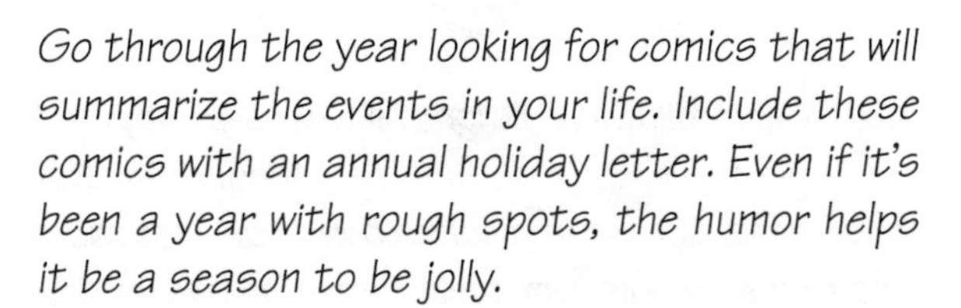

Go through the year looking for comics that will summarize the events in your life. Include these comics with an annual holiday letter. Even if it's been a year with rough spots, the humor helps it be a season to be jolly.

Two things reduce prejudice: education and laughter.

—*Laurence J. Peter*

How has laughter enlightened you about people who are different from you?

Recall the following anecdote whenever you find yourself locked in a conflict or difficult negotiation: A man is driving down a narrow mountain road and encounters another car coming up. The two can not pass. The first driver says, "I never back up for fools." The second driver says, "I always do," as he puts his car in reverse.

Comedy is like a muscle; if you don't use it, it begins to atrophy.

—*Jay Leno*

What are you going to do for your humor workout today?

Whenever you are bored, brainstorm a playful list of alternative activities, like hanging around the movies just to smell the popcorn or going through the fast-food drive-through three times in a row.

The whole object of comedy is to be yourself and the closer you get to that, the funnier you will be.

—*Jerry Seinfeld*

How would you describe the elf in yourself?

Leave yourself funny messages on your home answering machine. It's fun to listen to them after dinner.

Laughing is the only form of revolt we have in this country.

—Larry Klein

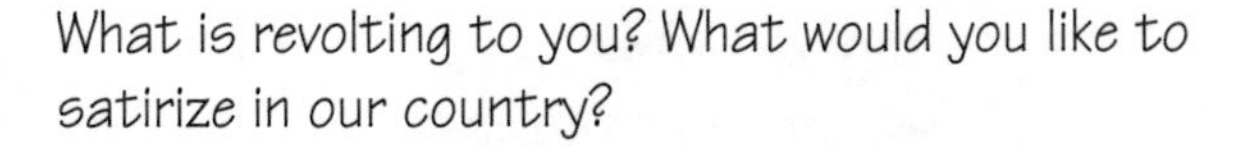

What is revolting to you? What would you like to satirize in our country?

Cut out Dave Barry and Art Buchwald columns and circulate them at work. (Dave surely will be delighted that Alert Readers are doing this!)

..SOMETIMES MY STOMACH LIKES TO RELIVE ITS CHILDHOOD !!
PEANUT BUTTER
GRAPE JELLY
MILK
ANIMAL CRACKERS
TOM WILSON

Jest . . . in case you're wondering what you want to be when you grow up.

—Joel Goodman

What do you want to be when (and if) you grow up?

Use the quote attributed to that wise old sage, Yogi Berra: "When you come to a fork in the road, take it!" It can help you and your organization to lighten up the load and the road when you face a difficult decision.

When I die and anyone thinks about it, rather than a moment of silence, I'd much prefer a moment of laughter.

—Bob Talbert

How would you like people to remember you? What are you doing about it now?

While mourning the loss of a dear person, have everyone tell of a funny event involving that person. Laughter can be a wonderful legacy.

Laughter removes chains and creates new freedom.

—Anaïs Nin

When have you experienced liberating laughter? How can you break out of your self-imposed shackles today?

Make up a card and hang it over your desk or put it on your refrigerator at home: "When you reach the end of your rope. . . hang on!"

You would hardly appreciate the comic if you felt yourself isolated from others. Laughter appears to stand in need of an echo.

—Henri Bergson

Who is a kindred comic spirit for you? How can you be in touch with that person today?

Friends and fun are two keys to a good laugh-life. Call old high school friends and share recent follies, foibles and embarrassments. It's a way of sharing "blasts from the present" with "blasts from the past."

There ain't much fun in medicine, but there's a heck of a lot of medicine in fun.

—Josh Billings

Celebrate National Nurses' Day: How do you nurse your own sense of humor? How can you inject fun into otherwise serious medical situations?

Serious illness is not a laughing matter. But sometimes you stumble across unintentional humor, like the medical record that stated, "Patient has been married twice, but denies any other serious illness."

For me, comedy is a tool. It's therapeutic for me. I use it as a release. You first start with yourself, making fun of yourself, then the world is open to you.

—Robin Williams

How can you jump-start your own sense of humor today?

Read the comics everyday before the front page, editorials and local news. Consciously try to find something that gives you an early-morning chuckle.

A joke's a very serious thing.

—Winston Churchill

How important is it for our leaders to have a sense of humor?

Give this quote to your administrator or supervisor at work: "Trying to manage people is like trying to herd cats."

My method is to take the utmost trouble to find the right thing to say, and then to say it with the utmost levity.

—George Bernard Shaw

Isn't "utmost" a funny-looking word? What are some other words that look "funny" to you?

Use words and phrases in mixed-up fashion, sometimes intentionally and sometimes not. Coin phrases like "Heimlich Remover." It's fun to come up with definitions for these new-found words and phrases.

The sadnesses of life—far from totally discouraging laughter—give rise to it.

—Steve Allen

How do you move from sadness to encouraging laughter? How can you rise to the occasion today?

Introduce an expression at your office that helps to reframe everyday stress into laughing matters. One daily motto could be: "If it's not funny, we make it funny!"

I love comedy. It's the only art form that's also a social grace.

—Paul Reiser

How can love and laughter grace your life today?

Keep a file of the creative and funny responses to questionnaires gathered over the years. One form asked for the applicant's name, age and sex. The first two questions raised no eyebrows. The third question generated the following answer: "Sex: Once in Jacksonville, Florida."

Damaging humor is often humor without insight. It is the cheap shot and insensitive. There is no challenge or real wit in it, no AHA! It leverages fear.

—Alexis Driscoll

In what ways could you respond the next time someone uses what you perceive to be damaging humor or cheap shots?

When someone is using oppressive put-down humor, simply say with tongue-in-cheek, "I resemble that statement!" This will playfully interrupt the behavior and will give the person who said it pause to think.

Humor gives life dimension and color. Humor widens the horizon and alters perspective.

—Marian Lenzen

What color is humor to you? How can you be a more colorful character today?

Keep a supply of lollipops on your desk next to the SMILE sign and a bottle of bubbles—these offer fun stress relief for any passers-by.

I believe in laughter. I think it is food for the soul.

—*Tommy Lasorda*

If you were to come up with a recipe for Humor Soul Food, what ingredients would you use to "make sense of humor"?

Contrary to what you were taught as a kid . . . play with your food. Set up a pie-throwing contest. Twist your ear as you zoop spaghetti into your mouth. Have a popcorn party. Go dunking for apples (even when it's not Halloween).

Every kid should have a joke-a-day to keep the glums away.

—Ann Bishop

What is your joke-of-the-day for today?

Purchase a variety of joke-of-the-day and cartoon-of-the-day calendars (e.g., Ziggy®, The Far Side®, or Dave Barry). Make it a playful goal to hand out the day's cartoon or joke to people you come across: clerks, gas station attendants, coworkers, friends and family.

My advice in the midst of the seriousness is to keep an eye out for the tinker shuffle, the flying of kites, and kindred sources of surprised amusement.

—Jerome Bruner

Can you do the tinker shuffle?

Go fly a kite.

Humor is not something just fun and frivolous. It is necessary and should be encouraged. Laughter is too good a thing to leave to chance. Laugh and pass it along.

—*Vera Robinson*

How has humor served you in the past? What are some of the benefits that you've experienced? How can you pass those benefits along to others?

If people in the office are taking themselves too seriously, take on the persona of "Reverend Will B. Dunn," and preach until the tension is broken and people break into laughter.

When the going gets tough, the smart get . . . laughing.

—Joel Goodman

How can you get your humor going today?

Collect cartoons that focus on different areas of life. For each area, create a cartoon album to help you not take life so seriously.

Humor comes from self-confidence.

—*Rita Mae Brown*

What do you feel confident about? What do you feel competent about?

Whenever you make a mistake, simply say, "I'm smarter now."

Humor is another of the soul's weapons in the fight for self-preservation. It is well known that humor, more than anything else in the human makeup, can afford an aloofness and an ability to rise above any situation, even if only for a few seconds.

—*Victor Frankl in* Man's Search for Meaning

What is a situation above which you would like to rise today? What would you see if you were above it all?

If your organization always seems to be in a state of change, then play with "change"—turn your boss' picture of Eisenhower upside-down and see how long it takes someone to notice; wear a shirt inside-out. Playing with change makes it less scary and less stressful.

Comedy is the last refuge of the non-conformist mind.

—Gilbert Seldes

What peer pressure do you feel most acutely? How can you use a light touch today to ward off this pressure to conform?

Engage in "brainstorming breaks" to recharge your batteries during the day. Think up nutty inventions (like ear deodorant) as a way of breaking set . . . and breaking the hold conformity may have on you.

To listen to your own silence is the key to comedy.

—Elayne Boosler

Where can you find some time for reflection today?

To remind yourself to minimize perfectionism while you strive for excellence, take 30 seconds to draw a self-portrait with your least-favored hand.

I think the next best thing to solving a problem is finding some humor in it.

—*Frank Clark*

Think of a challenge you're facing. What's so funny about it?

Where do all the missing socks in the universe go? At work, have lots of fun with a monthly Black Sock Exchange Day.

Well, I don't think much of giving advice, because most people don't listen anyway when they hear it. But I'll say this much—what's worked for us is to keep a good, healthy sense of humor and not take marriage or each other too seriously.

—Lucy VanDenburg on her 72nd wedding anniversary

What humorous advice would you give to another couple? What humorous advice would you give yourself in your own relationships?

The next time you read the fortune from a fortune cookie, just add the phrase, ". . . in bed" to the end of the fortune.

To laugh often and much, to win the respect of intelligent people and the affection of children . . . to leave the world a bit better . . . to know even one life had breathed easier because you have lived, that is to have succeeded.

—Ralph Waldo Emerson

What are you doing to leave the world a bit better?

Offer to do volunteer work for a hospital, nursing home, human service agency or school. Spread good cheer by reading humorous books to patients or students, by clowning, by George!

Laughter has no age. It belongs to all generations—especially when it's shared. That's the secret of crossing the generation gap.

—Bob Talbert

What other tips could you offer to bridge the generation gap?

With your parents, see how many years you can send the same birthday card back and forth between you.

Wit has truth in it; wisecracking is simply calisthenics with words.

—Dorothy Parker

What is one truth in your life that lends itself to laughter?

At work, open to any page in the dictionary and then use the words on that page to discuss the day with your staff or coworkers. This is a challenging—and fun—pop quiz that invites creativity and laughter.

We don't laugh because we're happy—we're happy because we laugh.

—William James

What invites laughter in your life today? What invites happiness? Where do the two intersect?

Carry a huge, stuffed animal with you. It will provide a fun excuse for people to hug, to lighten up and to grin and bear it!

Laughter binds us together in a kind of secret freemasonry.

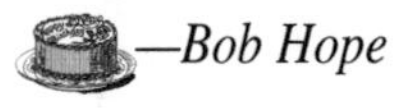
—Bob Hope

How can you connect with other people with laughter today?

Say something positive to the first sour-faced person you see each day. It inevitably breaks up his or her mindset into laughter.

God is a comedian playing to an audience that is afraid to laugh.

—*Voltaire*

What fears could laughter help you to embrace today?

When you're feeling up-tight and out-of-sorts, just say to yourself, "If it's not fatal, it's no big deal."

It has always surprised me how little attention philosophers have paid to humor since it is a more significant process of mind than reason. Reason can only sort out perceptions, but the humor process is involved in changing them.

—Edward de Bono

What is something in your life that you need to perceive differently today? How do you go about changing your world view?

In your organization, humor can often save the day (and week and month . . .). With your co-workers, coin such sayings as, "A mistake is just another way of doing things" and "Leadership can be defined by looking at your group—are they following you or chasing you?"

...SO I TAKE IT THAT OUR FIRST NIGHT OF OBEDIENCE SCHOOL DIDN'T GO AS WELL AS WE MIGHT'VE HOPED!
DUNCE
DUNCE
Tom Wilson

***Humor is laughter made from pain—
not pain inflicted by laughter.***

—Joel Goodman

How do you tell the difference between "laughing at others" and "laughing with others"?

Put up this notion on your bulletin board at work, on your blackboard at school or on your refrigerator at home: "You don't have to blow out my candle to make yours glow brighter." Use this statement as a stimulus for discussion.

Humor is counterbalance. Laughter need not be cut out of anything, since it improves everything.

—*James Thurber*

What is one part of your life that laughter could improve today?

Name your particularly fractious and difficult computer, "Bertha." Have everybody in the office bring her offerings. Celebrate both her birthday and anniversary (and occasionally plot her murder). This especially helps you to be up when your computer is down.

An epigram is a half-truth so stated as to irritate the person who believes the other half.

—Shailer Mathews

Can you create an epigram for yourself that will both irritate and amuse you?

Each week, type in a new quote or slogan under your letterhead that goes out on all of your correspondence, like "The best thing about being imperfect is the joy it brings to others."

Life is too serious to be taken seriously.

—Mike Leonard

What is something that you're taking too seriously? How can you let go of it today?

At work, start a club. No matter how often you're invited to join, always decline membership in the YTYTDS Club (You Take Yourself Too Darn Seriously).

Laughter is the most inexpensive and most effective wonder drug. Laughter is a universal medicine.

—Bertrand Russell

What directions should someone follow for this mirthful medicine? What can you do today to get a "natural high" from this wonder drug?

Each day, clip out your favorite comics from the newspaper. Put these comics together in a box. Whenever a friend is sick in bed or in the hospital, loan him or her the box.

Humor is your own smile surprising you in your mirror.

—Langston Hughes

What can you do today to surprise yourself?

Have lots of fun by putting up a sign in your office: KEEP RIGHT (with arrow pointing left).

Laughter sometimes comes out of very private tears.

—*Joan Rivers*

What is it that hurts you? Where will your laughter come from today?

Take a light look at self-fulfilling (or unfulfilling) prophecies: "When I'm feeling alone and depressed, a voice comes out of the gloom saying, 'Cheer up, things could be worse.' So I cheer up, and sure enough, things get worse."

I realize that humor isn't for everyone. It's only for people who want to have fun, enjoy life, and feel alive.

—Anne Wilson Schaef

Do you fit in any of the three categories above? What are you going to do about it?

Keep a goofy hat (or a Goofy hat) in your office. Whenever people are going off the wall, don the hat to help.

Jokes are always about things that are wrong. We laugh at our tragedies in order to prevent our suffering.

—Steve Allen

What's something wrong that you would like to fix in your life?

Make it a point to retell jokes you've heard—enough times (usually three or four) so you will remember them.

A merry heart doeth good like a medicine; but a broken spirit drieth the bones.

—Proverbs 17:22

Do you know someone whose spirit is broken? What merry medicine can you share with him or her?

Write (and send or give) prescriptions for fun to your friends, coworkers and family. And write some Rx's for yourself, too!

Joys shared are doubled, sorrows shared are halved.

—*Katherine Ferrari*

Who can you lean on? Who leans on you? Who can you laugh with?

Celebrate National Hug Day! Write treasure hunts for your children, nieces and nephews when they are looking for entertainment. The hunts could include activities like singing certain songs, giving hugs to parents, figuring out riddles—plus a small fun reward at the end.

If someone complains that punning is the lowest form of humor, you can tell them poetry is verse.

—Bob Davis

What poem speaks to you? Can you go from bard to verse?

Have fun with parody in verse. Make up new words to songs. Break up (literally and figuratively) long meetings or trips with this strategy.

A well-balanced person is one who finds both sides of an issue laughable.

—Herbert Prochnow

What is laughable about a conflict you are facing now?

Help people to see the humor in their situations by telling funny stories about things that have happened to you.

Comedians tell the world how important it is to laugh. When you laugh, you can't hate.

—Michael Pritchard

How do you think humor could be used to reduce prejudice, stereotyping and hatred in our world?

In the midst of a conflict, break the tension by using a saying like, "Never wrestle with a pig—you both get dirty, and the pig likes it."

Life is like laughing with a cracked rib.

—Peter McWilliams

What cracks you up? What do you like to be ribbed about?

Use a video camera to make your own version of America's Funniest Home Videos. *Your family and friends will appreciate the legacy of laughter captured in these videotapes. Every year, sit down to relive and relaugh.*

I deeply believe in humor; not in jokes. Humor is spectacular!

—Tom Peters

What are five ways other than jokes that you can invite smiles and laughter today?

Invite every department in your organization to contribute one funny anecdote each month to an employee newsletter. It's a great way to solicit and spread humor across the organization.

Humor plays close to the big, hot fire, which is the truth, and the reader feels the heat.

—*E.B. White*

What is something truthful you could say in jest today?

In your correspondence, always add a humorous postscript to leave 'em laughing.

Wit ought to be a glorious treat, like caviar; never spread it around like marmalade.

—Noel Coward

How can you use humor and wit the next time you're in a jam?

Place a jar of different-colored jellybeans on your desk along with a list of which color to take for each kind of stress.

Laughter is an instant vacation.

—*Milton Berle*

What kind of vacation can you plan that will really be fun for you?

Because it's often tough traveling long-distance with kids, invent funny games to play in the car, like transposing the first letters of first and last names. So, George Bush becomes Beorge Gush, Snow White becomes Whoa Snite, and so on.

An emotional person may possess no humor, but a humorous person usually has deep pockets of emotion.

—*Constance Roarke*

What moves you? What makes you laugh? Are they related?

When dealing with a difficult person on the phone, draw on your sense of humor and your emotional reserves—literally. Draw a caricature of the person to help you see some humor in the situation.

Humor is play that helps to tame the taboos.

—Daniel Juengst

What are your no-nos? How can you turn them into ho-hos?

Try to imagine obstacles as goals and write them as humorous proposals. This opens the door to creativity. For instance, you could lighten your load in going on a diet by writing a spoof purchase order for barbed wire to surround your refrigerator.

There is no jovial companionship equal to that where the jokes are rather small and the laughter abundant.

—Washington Irving

Can you think of a time that "a little thing" made a big difference?

When you go out with good friends, play a game of "It Was a Dark and Stormy Night." Each person in turn adds a line to the emerging story.

Laughter is the jest medicine.

—Joel Goodman

What can you do today to pay tribute to Norman Cousins on his birthday?

When someone you're with complains about growing old, you can kid, "Well, I hope your warranty hasn't run out!"

The biggest laughs are based on the biggest disappointments and the biggest fears.

—Kurt Vonnegut, Jr.

What's been a big disappointment for you in your life? Is it time to add some laughter?

At home or at the office, whenever negative thoughts outweigh the positive, use the phrase, "That's Stinkin' Thinkin'" to get yourself out of the rut.

Humor may be defined as the kindly contemplation of the incongruities of life and the artistic expression thereof.

—Steven Leacock

What doesn't fit in your life? How can the artist in you express this?

Inject humor in your presentations by including seemingly irrelevant facts to the audience at hand. For instance, one woman making a presentation about health care plans to senior citizens would tell about the maternity benefits available. She always got a laugh.

Don't be so full of adult—there is no room for the child in you.

—Bob Basso

What can you do today to invite the child in you to come out and play?

Parenting can be both the most stressful and most delightful job in the world. Tape record "someday we'll laugh about this" memories involving your kids. One woman later recorded a scene in a public restroom with her two-year-old son: she was washing her hands at the sink when she heard a woman saying loudly, "Oh dear, oh my goodness!" She turned around to see her son Peter's feet in the stall with a woman going to the bathroom. The mom had to coax him out. He had crawled under to watch. The mom was laughing so hard, she could barely crawl out of the bathroom herself.

JUNE 28

Humor is just another defense against the universe.

—*Mel Brooks*

What are you defensive about? How can you use humor to be proactive today?

Keep humor books, games and toys on your desk at work. When you need mental health breaks, they're right there. Also tuck funny things like cartoons away in drawers at home. At least when you're looking for something you've misplaced, you'll come across something funny.

In matters of humor, what is appealing to one person may be appalling to another.

—Mel Helitzer

In matters of the heart and hearty laughter, what appeals to you? What appalls you?

Have a dunking booth for managers and supervisors at your company picnics. It's a great way to raise fun and funds for local charities at the same time.

**A smile creates another smile.
A smile is the first step for humor to be possible.**

—Alex Port

What is the first step you need to take to have humor enter your life today?

Every now and then, have fun with your fellow workers by giving out a PMS Award (Positively Motivating Smile).

HOME FOR
THE
INCURABLY
OPTIMISTIC
TOM WILSON

Humor is a set of attitudes and skills that we can use to move from "grim and bear it" to "grin and share it."

—Joel Goodman

How can you move from grim to grin today?

Relieve stress by writing rap songs whose lyrics start with the titles of country western songs.

It takes all sorts of in and outdoor schooling to get adapted to my kind of fooling.

—*Robert Frost*

What kind of fooling do you like? What can you do to fool around today?

Have a backwards dinner with your children. One of you plans the menu and cooks dinner starting with dessert. This can be a foolish family ritual you all will enjoy and savor.

The most revolutionary act one can commit in our world is to be happy.

—Patch Adams

How can you bring happiness to others today?

Contribute money to a local hospital to help them establish a humor room, comedy cart or humor library for patients, family members and staff.

My way of joking is to tell the truth; it's the funniest joke in the world.

—George Bernard Shaw

What is the funniest joke you can remember?

Keep joke and cartoon books in your office for others to borrow. It's a fun safety valve and helps to minimize potential isolation.

A leader without a sense of humor is apt to be like the grass mower at the cemetery—he has lots of people under him, but nobody is paying him any attention.

—Bob Ross

What do you look for in a leader? What leadership qualities do you possess?

Give your boss or supervisor a sign for his or her door: Answers—$1.00. Correct Answers—$2.00. Blank Looks—Free.

Humor is a manifestation of creativity and leads to creativity.

—*Bob Samples*

How can you manifest your creative spirit and your sense of humor today?

Form a think-tank group of "Possibility Thinkers" at work. Meet weekly or monthly, share ideas and laugh a lot.

What Humor is, not all the Tribe of Logick-Mongers can describe.

—Jonathan Swift

Can you defy Swift and come up with a formula for humor (e.g., $E=MC^2$: Energy=Mirth x Creativity^2)?

Have fun going through the yellow pages looking for logical yet serendipitous connections between people's names and their occupations. You'll discover people like family physician Dr. Gene Poole.

Comedy is one of the few professions where you can profit from your shortcomings.

—Fred Willard

How can you turn your shortcomings from lemons into lemonade today?

Start a humorous "Hall of Shame" in your office. Include in it such incidents as this from a therapist: He was treating a patient by extolling the virtues of self-awareness . . . only to look down to discover that the zipper on his pants was down.

July 10

Humor expressed with a gentle smile or exuberant mirth is recreational therapy.

—*Eileen Jackson*

What can you do today to recreate and re-create yourself?

Get a book like The New Games Book *or* Playfair: Everybody's Guide to Noncompetitive Play. *Get together with friends or family for a medley of cooperative, fun, energizing ice-breakers.*

Buffoons who take themselves seriously are often the funniest of all.

—*David Rossie*

What can you do to goose yourself if you find that you're taking yourself too seriously?

Create your own spoof club or organization to laugh at buffoonery. Dr. Jim Boren did this when he founded the International Association of Professional Bureaucrats (Jim believes that bureaucracy is the epoxy that greases the wheels of progress).

You can turn painful situations around through laughter. If you can find humor in anything—even poverty—you can survive it.

—*Bill Cosby*

As you look into your crystal ball, do you anticipate any "turning points" in your life? How can humor be of help at the bends in the road up ahead?

Play comedy cassette tapes, like Will Rogers or Bill Cosby, to enliven your drive time to and from work each day. Arrive at work with a smile on your face, and return home that way in the evening.

Good humor is a philosophical state of mind. It seems to say to Nature that we take her no more seriously than she takes us.

—M. Dale Baughman

What do you see as the connection between Nature and human nature?

Tickle Mother Nature after She has tackled you. For instance, after a tornado took their house, one family put up a sign saying, "Gone with the Wind."

The best way to deal with imperfection is to laugh at it . . . especially if you don't plan to change it.

—Joyce Saltman

How do you balance accepting yourself . . . while trying to improve yourself? How can humor be the fulcrum for you?

Whenever a stressful situation or embarrassing moment occurs, say with enthusiasm, "Oh! What an opportunity for growth and learning!"

I won't grow up. I don't wanna wear a tie and a serious expression in the middle of July!

—Peter Pan

Do you want to be a groan-up or a grown-up? How can you rekindle your childlike qualities along the way?

Have fun sometime when you're in an elevator with a group of strangers. Just start making a speech to "my dearly beloved." This is especially effective in tall buildings.

After God created the world, He created man and woman. And then to keep the whole thing from collapsing, He created humor.

—*Ernie Hoberecht*

Can you recall a time you collapsed laughing? How can you relive that thrilling moment of yesteryear?

When you hit a point of real disagreement with someone else, switch into two characters to continue the argument—like Imelda Marcos in conflict with Donald Duck. The argument will collapse in a heap of humor.

A smile is a curve that sets everything straight.

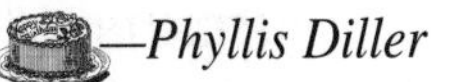

—*Phyllis Diller*

What is something that needs straightening out in your life? How can you draw on the funny line to help you?

When your friends or co-workers complain, tell them you'd be happy to share a little "whine" with them. It's a fun signal for all of you to lighten up.

I live by this credo: Have a little laugh at life and look around you for happiness instead of sadness. Laughter has always brought me out of unhappy situations. Even in your darkest moment, you usually can find something to laugh about if you try hard enough.

 —*Hats off to Red Skelton*

What is your credo? Have you had your little laugh today?

Look for funny hats in thrift shops. Wear them at work and act as though nothing is different as you go about your business.

A cardinal rule of humor: Never say anything about anyone that the person can't change in five seconds. Use the "AT&T" test for stories and jokes—make sure it's Appropriate, Timely and Tasteful.

—*Susan RoAne*

What acronym would you create to guide you in the positive use of humor?

Leave a humorous message on your answering machine. This encourages people to leave a message rather than to hang up. It's also a way to be more popular—you will certainly seem to get more phone calls.

A fun working environment is much more productive than a routine environment. People who enjoy their work will come up with more ideas. The fun is contagious.

—Roger Von Oech

What are three things you can do today to set in motion the contagion of fun?

Put up a bulletin board at work with pictures of staff in unusual situations with humorous sentences or newspaper headlines below the pictures. This sure will help you to see the humor in yourselves . . . literally.

Comedy is acting out optimism.

—Robin Williams

How can you act on your comedic optimism today?

For a committee of which you're a member, ask everyone to bring a cartoon or joke to share. Start the meeting with these contributions, which, in turn, can cheer you up before tackling the work at hand.

I once asked Edwin Arlington Robinson if he did not think his sense of humor had lengthened his life. "I think," he replied, "my life has lengthened my sense of humor."

—Daniel Gregory Mason

How has your sense of humor developed and stretched over the years?

To celebrate a friend's birthday, rent a stretch limo for an hour for the two of you to ride around in.

What I want to do is to make people laugh so that they'll see things seriously.

—William K. Zinsser

What's something you laugh about in your life about which you are also serious?

Advise your staff and fellow workers that "boss" spelled backwards is double SOB. Instead of sobs, this can invite laughter.

Comedy is an ability to observe and see what's funny in a situation and be able to forget yourself enough to do it.

—Madeline Kahn

What is the key for you to be able to "forget"—to let go and give yourself permission to be playful?

Make a placard: "Don't take everything so seriously! Smile and give your face a break!"

God cannot be solemn, or He would not have blessed humans with the incalculable gift of laughter.

—Sydney Harris

What are the blessings that your sense of humor has given you?

Keep a journal of "humorous grace under fire." Here's an example: During exams for a theology class in Southern California, there was an earthquake. The professor had stepped out of the room prior to the shake. After it stopped, he walked back into the room and asked with a smile, "Which one of you is trying to cheat?!"

Like a welcome summer rain, humor may suddenly cleanse and cool the earth, the air and you.

—Langston Hughes

How is your humor these days—all dried up . . . a drizzle . . . a steady rain . . . a downpour?

Every now and then, ask a question that mirrors or slightly modifies another person's statement. This often helps to break the ice by rerouting the person's mind set. For example, one patient was wet and cried, "I'm sorry!" The nurse smiled and asked, "Did you say 'I'm sorry' or 'I'm soggy'?" The patient smiled and said, "I'm sorry I'm soggy." The laughter that followed was cleansing for both of them.

JULY 27

Humor keeps you in the present. It is very difficult to laugh and be disassociated with the people around you. In that one moment together you have unity and a new chance.

—Alexis Driscoll

How do you stay in the precious present? What are your strategies for centering yourself? How can humor help you in this?

Spend an hour in the presence of a young child. Follow the child's whim. This will encourage you to stay in the present.

The more you share your happiness with others, the more you have yourself.

—Maxwell Maltz

How much happiness can you give away today?

Clip as many Reader's Digest jokes and anecdotes as you can find. Then tape them to index cards and hand them out to people who need a lift. It's fun being a card-carrying card!

On a throne at the center of a sense of humor sits a capacity for irony. All wit rests on a cheerful awareness of life's incongruities. It is a gentling awareness, and no politician without it should be allowed near power.

—*George Will*

What will you do today to pump irony?

Keep joke books in your informal library—the bathroom. Starting the day with your "humor library" is a great way to get a royal flush of laughter.

Humor allows for a boundary between where we are and some of the cruel things that happen to us.

—Joseph Steiner

How can you use humor to protect yourself and your self-esteem today?

Each day, take to the office a mug that fits your mood of the day . . . or that can help you break out of the mood, like "The next thing you say may be what puts me completely over the edge."

Among animals, one has a sense of humor. Humor saves a few steps, it saves years.

—*Marianne Moore*

When has humor saved you over the years?

Give your pet a fun name or nickname. One man named his dog, "What?" He loved it when people asked him the dog's name. It was doggone funny!

...AND WHY DID YOU LEAVE YOUR JOB AS AN ELEVATOR OPERATOR?
PERSONNEL
Tom Wilson

God grant me the serenity to accept the things I cannot change, the courage to change the things I can, the wisdom to know the difference . . . and the sense of humor when I don't know the difference.

—Joel Goodman adding to Reinhold Niebuhr

Where and how do you draw the line between the things you cannot change and those you can?

The next time you don't know where you are (figuratively), say the words, "Gee, Toto, I don't think we're in Kansas anymore!"

Laughter is a celebration of the human spirit.

—Sabina White

What's one thing you can do today to lift your own and others' spirits?

Plan fun contests for your family and company picnics—like having a contest blowing up balloons. The winner is clearly full of hot air.

Nature itself gives us musculature by which we perform an act called "a smile," and physical equipment by which we perform another act called "laughing".

—Steve Allen

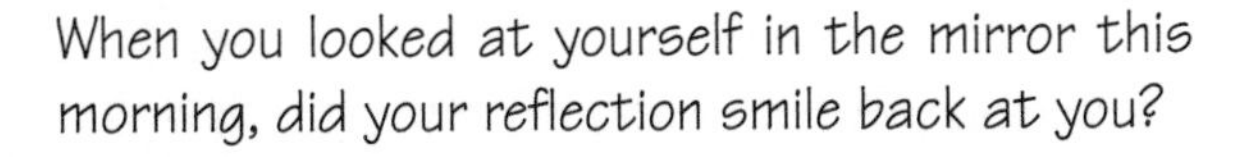

When you looked at yourself in the mirror this morning, did your reflection smile back at you?

When your children are annoyed about something and are pouting, say to them, "Don't you dare smile!" It always works—not only will they smile, they'll usually end up laughing out loud.

Gaff and the world laughs with you.

—Aaron Abbott

Are you willing to stick your neck out enough to make mistakes . . . and to laugh at yourself in the process?

When you are late for a meeting, have fun making up ridiculous, creative excuses for your tardiness.

So long as there's a bit of a laugh going, things are all right. As soon as this infernal seriousness, like a greasy sea, heaves up, everything is lost.

—D.H. Lawrence

How can you keep your laughter going in the face of adversity?

On occasion, write a spoof memo calling for more humor on Tuesdays and Thursdays in your otherwise serious office.

Humor is not a trick, not jokes. Humor is a presence in the world—like grace—and shines on everybody.

—Garrison Keillor

What are some of the humor tricks-of-the-trade you use to keep humor shining on you?

Celebrate Garrison Keillor's birthday by celebrating your own mirthday! Create your own monologue from Lake Wobegon to help you maintain your humor presence in the world.

They that are serious in ridiculous things will be ridiculous in serious affairs.

—Cato the Elder

Are you serious in ridiculous things? Are you ridiculous in serious things? Are you ridiculous in ridiculous things?

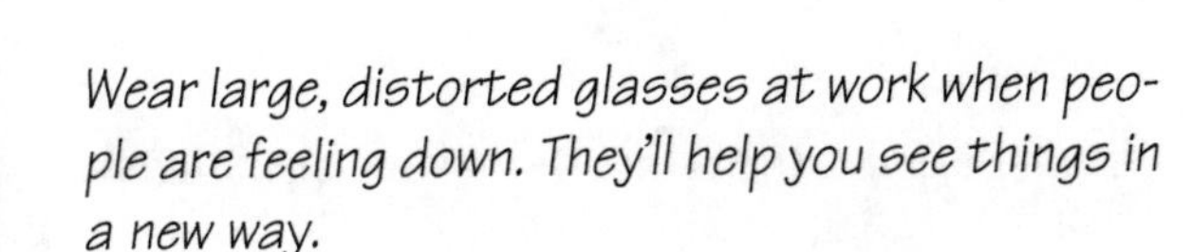

Wear large, distorted glasses at work when people are feeling down. They'll help you see things in a new way.

If you understand what makes a people laugh, you are closer to understanding and appreciating them.

—Joe Bruchac

How are you humorous? How would an observer describe you when you are your most humorous self?

Begin asking others what makes them laugh. When they answer, you both may end up laughing.

You can only laugh if you can cry.

—Tomie de Paola

How deep is your emotional well today?

Reminisce about previous good times. Walking (and skipping) down memory lane in this way can bring out funny stories, tears and laughter.

Laughter is, after speech, the chief thing that holds society together.

—*Max Eastman*

What is the chief thing that holds you together?

During coffee breaks, try to break each other up by saying things like, "Need help with the computer? Here's a hammer!"

Anything worth taking seriously is worth making fun of.

—*Tom Lehrer*

What subject is worthy of your humor?

When people are taking themselves and their relationships too seriously, read humorous personal want ads aloud to one another.

Lots of laughter and a sprinkling of love—as far as we know, that's the best way to deal with anyone.

—Lynne Alpern and Esther Blumenfeld

With whom do you laugh the most? What is it about that person that "invites" you to laugh?

To help your family start the day on the light side of the bed, play a particular funny tape or CD to wake them up. Music amuses and is a fun wake-up call.

What is comedy? Comedy is the art of making people laugh without making them puke.

—*Steve Martin*

Where do you draw the line when it comes to sick humor?

Have fun with your friends. Secretly put a piece of lemon peel over your upper front teeth and then smile broadly at your companion as you sit down to lunch.

I have always felt that laughter in the face of reality is probably the finest sound there is and will last until the day when the game is called on account of darkness. In this world, a good time to laugh is any time you can.

—Linda Ellerbee

Is this a good time to laugh? If not now, when?

In the middle of Winter, arrange with several neighboring families to squirrel away a stockpile of snowballs in your freezers. Then, during the dog days of August, have a giant snowball fight.

Humor is the sense of the absurd which is despair refusing to take itself seriously.

—Arland Ussher

How can you move from despair to humor to hope today?

Join an "out-to-lunch" support group. Get together each day (or week or month) for lunch and swap jokes and crazy things that have happened. It sure helps to digest your food . . . and the rest of reality.

When a thing is funny, search it for a hidden truth.

—George Bernard Shaw

What do you see when you look beyond laughter?

Collect cartoons about particular professions and send them to friends and family in those professions. Consider the cartoon of a surgeon saying to a patient, "I'm afraid we won't know the exact nature of your condition until after the autopsy."

This I conceive to be the chemical function of humor: to change the character of our thought.

—*Lin Yutang*

How can humor help you transform your thinking today?

The next time your boss gives you grief, just visualize him or her as Big Bird. The feathers in your mind will tickle your funnybone.

An optimist laughs to forget; a pessimist forgets to laugh.

—Tom Nansbury

What can you do to remind yourself to laugh today?

Purchase a Ziggy® calendar with a funny cartoon for each day. Share the cartoon-of-the-day with everyone in your office or family—especially during grim times.

Humor is the contemplation of the finite from the point of view of the infinite.

—Christian Morgenstern

Where does your view of the cosmos and your view of the comic intersect?

During times of stress, send your coworkers a memo that has the heading, "The difference between this place and the Titanic is that the Titanic had a band."

The value of being able to laugh at ourselves when we make a mistake: it helps us get on with our work.

—*Ken Blanchard*

What's one mistake you can make today that's laughable?

Each day, make up a new sign for your desk that will bring a chuckle from people who come into your office. For example, "Please solve your problems in advance so I can help you faster."

Humor is the instinct for taking pain playfully.

—Max Eastman

No play, no gain. What have you played with today?

Whenever there is enough tension in the room that you could cut it with a knife, just start singing. That usually clears the air (and the room) quickly.

Humor is surprise, a sharp, 90-degree turn. Life is just one predictable thing after another, one monotonous road if you allow it to be. But with humor, all of a sudden you're on the dodge-'em cars.

—*Mark Russell*

What's a metaphorical dodge-'em car that you can ride today? How can you surprise yourself?

Every now and then, be off-the-wall playful in order to survive emotionally. Take a boring task and do it differently, like putting the groceries away alphabetically.

Among those whom I like, I can find no common denominator; but among those whom I love, I can: all of them make me laugh.

—*Wystan Auden*

Whom do you love? Who loves you? What do you have in common?

Fax funny pictures to your friends and colleagues in other offices. The headline above each one is "The FAX of Life."

A comedian's job is to make people laugh. But a humorist makes them laugh and then think. Humor is a way of life, a pattern of behaving. It's the ability to bend without breaking. Humor is like a diaper change—it makes you comfortable for awhile. Take life seriously, but not mournfully.

—*M. Dale Baughman*

Beware of that dreaded disease, rectal opticalis. Have you changed your diaper today?

At the entrance to your office, have an "Oasis" board on which you put funny cartoons. Invite others to add their cartoons. The sign on the board is, "Grins and Gripes." This will help you to keep track of what's happening—an informal balance sheet of smiles and frowns.

Wit is the sudden marriage of ideas which before their marriage were not perceived to have any relationship.

—*Mark Twain*

What surprises you? Where can you look for surprises today?

In social settings, do the unexpected; set a table with fine china and use a sneaker as the centerpiece.

Good humor is goodness and wisdom combined.

—Owen Meredith

What is a good deed that you could perform today? How about letting somebody get in line in front of you at the grocery store?

Tape jokes, quotes and cartoons near a pay telephone, like "Smile when you say 'Hello'!" It's fun to give a bit of lightness to strangers who use the phone. It's also fun to see their reactions.

Mark my words, when a society has to resort to the lavoratory for its humor, the writing is on the wall.

—*Alan Bennett*

If you had a graffiti board, what would you put on it?

At your office, place a plaque in one of the bathroom stalls that reads, "Smile, You're On Candid Camera." You'll always be able to tell when a visitor goes to the bathroom.

The major role of jokes, after all, is to make us laugh while cleverly pointing out ways in which reality makes mincemeat of conventional wisdom.

—*William Zachmann*

What is the major role of humor in your life?

Jest . . . in case you hate housework. Put up a sign or find a bumper sticker that says something like, "The only thing domestic about me is the fact that I live in a house."

It is very hard to sustain humor, or the desire for humor, in a period when we seem to be trying, on the one hand, to invent a pill or a miracle drug that will cure us of everything, and on the other to invent machines for instant annihilation.

—James Thurber

How can you sustain your own spirit today? How can you maintain your desire for humor?

Whenever things get too grim in your organization, start rolling in the aisles—put on your roller blades and take a tour around the office.

Comedy is a distraction, not an action. Humor takes your mind off the negative and turns it into laughter that's positive.

—*Buddy Hackett*

What do you need to take your mind off? What do you need to put your mind to today?

Allow yourself to be in the moment and see the humor in each little thing that happens. Humor is there all the time; taking time and space to experience it will help you to laugh more.

HEY!...
WHAT HAPPENED
TO THE
CARROT CAKE?

People with a good sense of humor are part of the greatest show on mirth.

—Joel Goodman

Where did you get your sense of humor?

Create your own mirth-aid kit. Hang a basket of fun props and toys near your desk or the receptionist's desk to use when you or your coworkers need a laugh break.

He deserves paradise who makes his companions laugh.

—*The Koran*

Who makes you laugh? How do they do it?

In your office, alter comics from the newspaper to fit your organization—your cast of characters (in the office) can choose their alter-ego cartoon characters (Charlie Brown, Beetle Bailey, Cathy, Ziggy and so on).

Dying is easy. Comedy is difficult.

—*Edmund Gwenn*

How can you administer CPR (Comedy Pulmonary Resuscitation) to yourself? How can you revive your sense of humor when it's dying?

While in the midst of a stressful situation, give funny cards to friends, family or coworkers—like the card that shows two fish swimming in a blender with the caption, "I can't stand the tension!"

Humor is a very important part of a marriage. Sometimes you have to break the tension with a joke or a look.

—Bob Newhart

What nonverbal cues tell you that you're in trouble with your spouse? What nonverbal cues could you use to help lighten up the situation?

The next time you're going on a business trip alone, leave a joke or cartoon on your spouse's pillow.

Humor is perhaps a sense of intellectual perspective: an awareness that some things are really important, others not; and that the two kinds are most oddly jumbled in everyday affairs.

—Christopher Morley

What is important to you? How can you get more of it? What is not important to you? How can you let go of it?

Use dry humor to summarize a stressful situation—for example, "We've been waiting all our lives for this. . . ."

When you discard arrogance, complexity and a few other things that get in the way, sooner or later you will discover that simple, childlike and mysterious secret . . . Life is Fun.

—*Benjamin Hoff,* The Tao of Pooh

What secrets have you discovered today?

Get a lot of humor in your life just by going over to the local recreation field and watching five-year-olds play soccer!

Comedy has to be truth. You take the truth and you put a little curlicue at the end.

—*Sid Caesar*

How can you add a curlicue to your reality today?

In your office, set up a humor bulletin board that features "The Rumor of the Week." A tongue-in-cheek rumor can lead to humor—and humor keeps us up as we look at what's going down.

Comedy is allied to justice.

—*Aristophanes*

What is the connection between "just" and "jest"?

Listen to the dual meanings of words and use them to lighten up otherwise serious situations. For instance, when the insurance claims adjuster asks, "Where was the mailman bitten?", jest say, "On the porch."

Prepare for mirth, for mirth becomes a feast.

—William Shakespeare

What can you do to bring mirth to your meals today?

Eat a lot of Chinese food! Tape fortune cookie fortunes to your bathroom mirror at home and at your desk at work to remind yourself to lighten up.

Even if laughter were nothing more than sheer silliness and fun, it would still be a precious boon. But we now know that it is far more than that, that it is, in fact, an essential element in emotional health.

—Steve Allen

What can you do today just for the sheer silliness and fun of it?

Have fun by taking language literally. Tell someone to meet you at "7:00 on the dot." At 7 o'clock, put a dot on the floor where you're supposed to meet.

Humor is the harmony of the heart.

—*Douglas Jerrold*

How can you play with your humor today to create harmonious connections with others' hearts?

Read a joke to your kids before they go to school. Start their day (and yours) with a smile.

A chuckle a day may not keep the doctor away but it sure makes those times in life's waiting room a little more bearable.

—Anne Wilson Schaef

How can you move from "killing time" to "enlivening time" today?

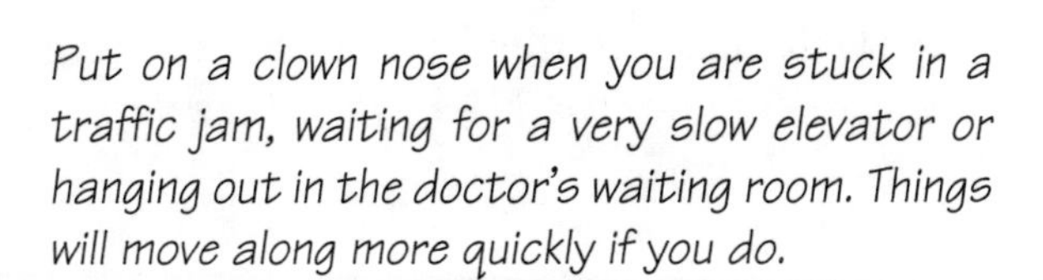

Put on a clown nose when you are stuck in a traffic jam, waiting for a very slow elevator or hanging out in the doctor's waiting room. Things will move along more quickly if you do.

Laughter loves company even more than misery loves company.

—Joel Goodman

Which contagion do you want to set in motion—misery or laughter?

Create a ritual that at 4:55 on Friday, someone plays "Heigh-Ho" (from Snow White) with a tape recorder or over the intercom system. Leave 'em laughing—as they head home for the weekend.

Red Skelton laughs a lot. That's because he loves life. As he says, "Life is wonderful. Without it, you're dead."

—Cliff Radel

What would your life be like without laughter?

Start your day with a three-minute laugh. This will get your blood circulating, the oxygen flowing and your face glowing. Look at yourself in the mirror . . . if that helps.

Comedy is the most serious study in the world. The best situations . . . the funniest will be an exaggeration of an action in real life which was not at all funny in itself.

—Charlie Chaplin

Is there some molehill in your life that you can make into a mountain of mirth?

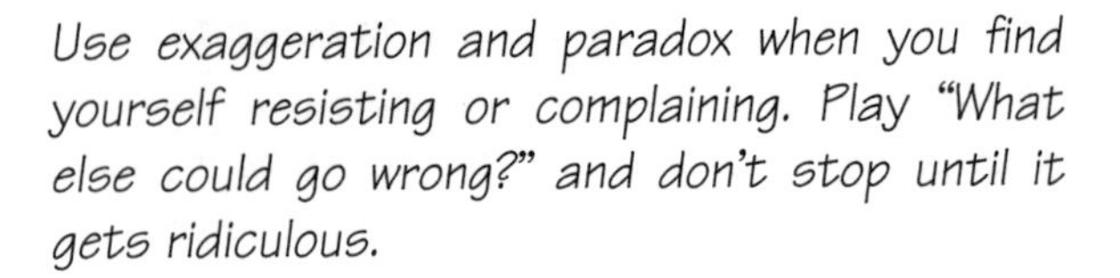

Use exaggeration and paradox when you find yourself resisting or complaining. Play "What else could go wrong?" and don't stop until it gets ridiculous.

There's a correlation between bad times and the rise of comedy. People need the escape.

—*David Brenner*

What would you like to escape from? Where would you like to escape to with humor?

Let go of the frustration of dealing with folks who have owed you money. Just entertain the thought of including the following note with statements to long-overdue customers: "Please pay us soon! It's been over nine months; we've carried you longer than your mother!"

Laughter and crying are two of the best healers we have.

—*Peter McWilliams*

How can you use laughter and tears as a soul-salve today?

When things get stressful, exaggerate the stress and laugh at it to keep it from having power over you.

The richest laugh is at no one's expense.

—*Linda Loving*

What is your least favorite kind of humor? What don't you like about it?

The next time someone uses hurtful humor, try to interrupt it by making an "I" statement and talking from your heart.

To be wildly enthusiastic or deadly serious—both are wrong. One must keep ever present a sense of humor.

—Katherine Mansfield

When do you find yourself to be dead serious? Serious? Dead?

Wear a tee shirt with a fun, tongue-in-cheek statement like, "Everyone is entitled to my opinion."

Humor provides us with a valuable tool for maintaining an inner strength in the midst of outer turmoil.

—*Brian Deery*

How can you use humor today to keep your balance?

In the midst of an insane situation, tape a note on your office door: "Why be normal?" People will smile as they enter. And you'll smile as you exit.

The art of medicine consists of amusing the patient while nature cures the disease.

—*Voltaire*

What amuses you?

Have a "mental health day" policy in your organization. One day each year, you can "call in well" when you're feelin' good and want to take advantage of it.

People are endowed with a sense of humor as an antidote to alleviate the incongruities of life.

—*Steve Gioia*

Which puzzle piece does not fit in your life?

In reading the daily newspaper, look for incongruities, puns or double entendre headlines. For instance, there was a story about a skull found in the road; the headline was, "What's in the Road—A Head?"

When people are laughing, they're generally not killing one another.

—Alan Alda

How can you "kill somebody" with kindness and comedy today?

Whenever controversial issues arise at meetings, pass out rubber animal noses . . . as a playful way for you to disagree without being disagreeable.

Laughter is free, legal, has no calories, no cholesterol, no preservatives, no artificial ingredients, and is absolutely safe.

—Dale Irvin

How can you free up and preserve your laughter?

Whenever you host a party, wrap cartoons or fortune cookies in the guests' dinner napkins. It's always fun to share the cartoons or fortunes with the others present.

Humor is looking at truth through distorted lenses.

—Max Shulman

Can you do the twist today—with humor?

Conspire with a couple of out-of-state friends to send each other the most bizarre and out-of-mind greeting cards you can find.

Frame your mind to mirth and merriment, which bar a thousand harms and lengthen life.

—William Shakespeare

What kind of mind-set or mind-un-set do you need to prepare for mirth and merriment today?

Carry a picture in your wallet of you and your dog (or someone else's dog) both wearing Groucho glasses. You will always get a laugh when you show it to others.

To become conscious of what is horrifying and to laugh at it is to become master of that which is horrifying.

—Eugene Ionesco

What horrifies you in this world? How could humor come to your rescue?

Buy—or make—buttons to wear under your lapel, like the one that says, "Was today really necessary?" You can "flash" your buttons to each other like an FBI agent would show a badge . . . as a humor-badge-of-courage to help you face the horrific.

Stand-up comedy is the bungee-jumping of the world of communications.

—*Michael Mendrick*

What could you do today to take a flying leap with humor?

Use props to prop-erly transmit humor in the office. For instance, put a battery on a plaque and give it as an award to an employee who was very energetic this week. Keep a hard hat in the office, too; anyone who's having a bad day can wear it . . . and invite some support and smiles at the same time.

Humor is a wonderful gift for living with our imperfection. Humor is the synapse between the perfection we seek and the imperfection we have.

—*Joel Goodman*

How can you give yourself the gift of humor today to lift the yoke/joke of perfectionism?

Keep things in perspective by having a poster in your office—like the one showing a galaxy and an arrow pointing to a little speck of light. The arrow says, "You are here."

YOU ARE HERE
BUT EVERYONE ELSE IS OVER HERE !!
X
X
Tom Wilson

A clown is like aspirin, only he works twice as fast.

—*Groucho Marx*

What can you do today to invite the Bozo in you to come out and work for you?

Join one of the clown ministry groups that have developed to use humor and mime in worship services at churches and synagogues (or create your own clown ministry troupe).

You must play the fool a little if you would not be thought wholly a fool.

—Michel de Montaigne

What do you do to fool around?

Entertain yourself fabulously when driving by singing Pete Seeger folk songs in operatic style with a Swedish accent.

To itself a lemon isn't sour; to a polecat, itself it doesn't stink. Before you try what to you is funny, take time to see what others think.

—*Richard Pope*

What puts a smile on the faces of others today?

Collect jokes and cartoons. Number them and give one to your boss each day. In serious meetings, your coworkers can refer to Joke #__ to break the tension.

If you watch a game, it's fun. If you play it, it's recreation. If you work at it, it's golf.

—Bob Hope

How can you build more fun and recreation into the game of life?

Keep a couple of small wind-up toys on your desk. When you are talking business with someone, encourage your visitor to pick one up the toys and play with it. This will automatically change the tone of the interaction.

October 6

One horse-laugh is worth 10,000 syllogisms. It is not only more effective; it is also vastly more intelligent.

—H.L. Mencken

One horse-laugh can result from 10,000 sillygisms. What's something you can do today to horse around that's just plain silly?

If things are tense at the dinner table, pick up the salt shaker and start to lip-synch with it. It will help you to take the situation at hand with a grain of salt.

A person without a sense of humor is like a wagon without springs—jolted by every pebble in the road.

—*Henry Ward Beecher*

What are some of the pebbles in your road? How can you add some spring to your life?

Whenever you are stressed out on the job, just say to yourself the following phrase to help you keep on going: "If I can just make it to the border. . . ."

Humor has a lot to do with perspective and giving people perspective.

—*Chevy Chase*

What is one new way of looking at an old problem you've been facing?

Put up a poster behind your desk that reads, "Do not interrupt me—I have already changed my mind."

The laughter in our home is its heart beating. Laughter leads us, kneads us and sometimes helps bleed us of torments and woes.

—Bob Talbert

What can you do to pass the legacy of laughter on to young people today?

Put funny notes in your children's school lunch boxes and under their pillows at night.

The person who sees the consistency in things is a wit; the person who sees the inconsistency in things is a humorist.

—G.K. Chesterton

What do you see when you look at the world—consistencies or inconsistencies?

Play with words and phrases; try to find phrases that are opposites and yet have the same meaning, like "slim chance" and "fat chance."

Humor is something that thrives between a person's aspirations and his limitations. There is more logic in humor than in anything else. Because, you see, humor is truth.

—*Victor Borge*

What are your big dreams in life? What are your big obstacles? Where is your belly laugh?

Cut out comic strips and clip them to the front of your appointment book so that you can share them with the people you meet . . . and so you can see humor on a daily basis.

There are enough tragedies in life; we have to have some laughs.

—*Steve Allen*

How did someone you know use humor to overcome a tragedy? What can you learn from this person?

When things are at their worst, just say to yourself, "When does the fun start?"

Then I commend mirth because a person hath no better thing under the sun than to eat, and to drink, and to be merry. . . .

—Ecclesiastes 8:15

How can you nurture your merry old soul today?

Start a weekly Staff Laff session over lunch. On a rotating basis, have each staff member take a turn preparing a meal. Relax and enjoy one another's company at the company.

OCTOBER 14

Humor is the great thing, the saving thing, after all. The minute it crops up, all our hardnesses yield, all our irritations and resentments slip away, and a sunny spirit takes their place.

—*Mark Twain*

What can you do to bask in your sunny spirit today?

Smile a lot, and just hand out imaginary smiles to anyone in need. It never fails!

Wit consists in knowing the likeness of things that differ, and the difference of things that are alike.

—Madame de Stael

What are the differences and similarities for you among wit, humor, comedy?

Put up a sign on your desk that reads, "It's hard to be a Monday person in a Friday world."

Life is too important to be taken seriously.

—*Oscar Wilde*

How can you import humor into those matters that are important to you?

At the office, use a running gag line: "I may have my faults, but being wrong is not one of 'em."

Many a true word is spoken in jest.

—English Proverb

Have you ever heard someone say, "To be perfectly honest with you . . ."? What would it feel like if they completed the sentence with an appreciation of you? Can you do this for someone else?

Leave silly—and supportive—messages on friends' answering machines.

A laugh is worth a hundred groans in any market.

—*Charles Lamb*

How can you turn groans into laughs today?

On the way to work, listen for the worst joke on morning radio; during the day share it with fellow employees.

I know what got me into comedy . . . Puberty!

—*Phyllis Diller*

In looking back at those thrilling days of yester-decade, what humor did you find in puberty?

In your family, if you ever encounter the "Not Me" phenomenon—if there is a mess on the floor and the kids all say "Not me. I didn't do it."—write notes addressed to "Not Me." The kids will get the point . . . and laugh, too.

Nobody can teach you humor writing. The secret is passed on from one generation to another and I will not tell mine, except to my son.

—*Art Buchwald*

What secrets about humor will you pass on to the next generation?

Before going to bed each night, write funny commercials that are take-offs on reality. It beats counting sheep.

True humor springs not more from the head than from the heart; it is not contempt, its essence is love; it issues not in laughter, but in still smiles which lie far deeper.

—*Thomas Carlyle*

Where is your humor spring? How does your humor present itself on the surface?

Keep a "Smile File" or a "Tickler File"—a file folder filled with funnies you've found over the years.

To be playful and serious at the same time is possible, and it defines the ideal mental condition.

—John Dewey

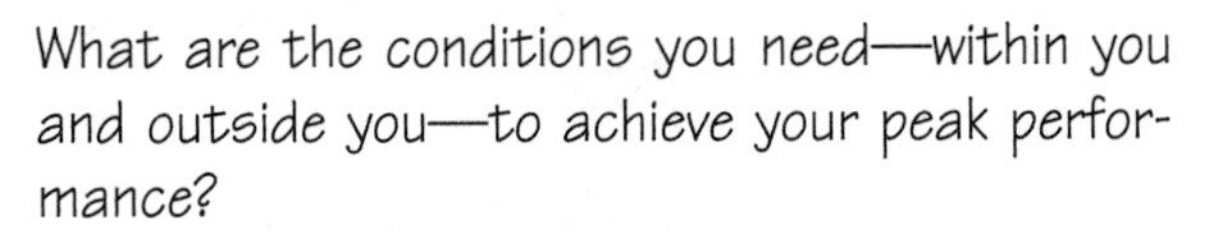

What are the conditions you need—within you and outside you—to achieve your peak performance?

Create a peak-a-bag ritual at your regular meetings. Each staff member brings in a favorite cartoon of the week and puts it in a bag. When moving from one agenda item to the next, pull out one of the cartoons, read it and try to guess which person brought it.

People will pay more to be entertained than educated.

—Johnny Carson

When have you experienced joy in learning? What is something you would enjoy learning more about?

Have your organization bring in outside speakers for inservice programs on humor in the workplace—a great chance for you to laugh and learn . . . individually and collectively!

Comedy comes out of exposing the difficulties in life and laughing at them.

—Louie Anderson

What part of your life would you like to expose . . . to humor?

Whenever a serious situation hits the office, break the tension by saying, "Film at 11:00."

Imagination was given to us to compensate for what we are not; a sense of humor was provided to console us for what we are.

—Mack McGinnis

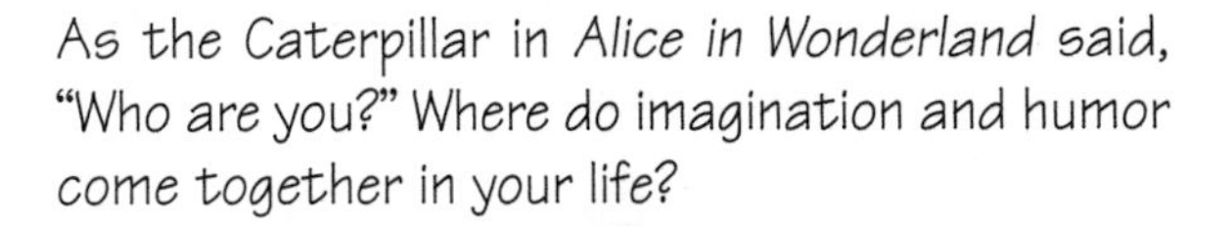

As the Caterpillar in *Alice in Wonderland* said, "Who are you?" Where do imagination and humor come together in your life?

Try to encourage a sense of wonder by helping people laugh at their fears. To support their curiosity, post a sign that says, "Make an ASK out of yourself—the only DUMB question is the question you do not ask."

What is unspeakably irritating today may well be tomorrow's funny story. So have a good laugh today!

—Nancy Comiskey

Have you ever had irritable vowel syndrome? How can you give voice (and laughter) to the unspeakable today?

When you're in a jam, pretend you're a comedian describing your situation to an audience.

If I can get you to laugh with me, you like me better, which makes you more open to my ideas.

—*John Cleese*

What is your process for opening up? How could you use humor to minimize resistance?

In your organization, give new employees a tongue-in-cheek taste for your corporate culture by telling them your motto: "You don't have to be inept to work here—we'll train you!"

Laughing is the sensation of feeling good all over and showing it principally in one spot.

—Josh Billings

Where is your laughing spot? How can you tickle it today?

Create a humor corner in your home or a humor room at your place of work. This is where you can go if you need a five-minute recharging of your batteries. Have fun dressing up this spot with a variety of amusements.

Humor is really laughing off a hurt, grinning at misery.

—Bill Mauldin

How can you tickle a hurt before it tackles you today?

Have fun concocting running jokes at the family dinner table—like the phrase, "You're interfering with my interrupting!"

Comedy is a way of thinking about the world. When you stop laughing, comedy really does make you think.

—*Ejner Jensen*

What do you think about the world? What in the world do you laugh about?

Purchase a Rolodex™ and turn it into a rolling-in-the-aisles-dex. Write humorous or motivational sayings on each card and file them alphabetically by topic. It's great to flip through when you're on hold.

I was wise enough to never grow up while fooling most people into believing I had.

—*Margaret Mead*

What would you like to be today?

Have all the staff (including administrators) come to work in costume on Halloween—it's a fun way to play at work.

...THIS IS ZIGGY SPEAKING... IF YOU WISH TO SPEAK TO MY ANSWERING MACHINE, LEAVE A MESSAGE AND IT'LL GET BACK TO YOU SHORTLY!!
Tom Wilson

Comic perspective leads to cosmic perspective—bringing humanity and sanity to inhumane and insane situations.

—Joel Goodman

How can humor help you feel most human *and* humane today?

Whenever you and your friends are facing a disastrous situation, make up lyrics to the tune of Don't Worry, Be Happy.

Humor is a divine quality and God has the greatest sense of humor of all—He must have, otherwise He wouldn't have made so many politicians.

—Martin Luther King

Would you support Presidential candidate James Boren, whose motto is "I've got what it takes to take what you've got!"?

Toss around mirthful mottoes to set a lighter tone in the workplace—like, "Humor knows no hierarchy," and "Don't take things too seriously, because by tomorrow they may not be important!"

We are all here for a spell. Get all the good laughs you can.

—*Will Rogers*

How many good laughs can you get today? Where will you look for them?

Take photos at formal events; later, draw in balloons and make up people's "thoughts."

Levity is the soul of wit.

—Melville Landon

How can you use levity to defy gravity today?

Use copyright-free clip art or cartoons on transparencies to illustrate points when you make presentations. Cartoons seem to "help the medicine go down."

Humor has always been an expression of the freedom of the human spirit. It is an ability to stand outside of life's flow and view the whole scene—the incongruities, the tragedies outside our control, the unexpected.

—Terry Paulson

What playful title would you give your own autobiography?

When things get really hectic, try to step back and view your life as a situation comedy.

Without laughter, the spiritual path would be boring.

—Alan Cohen

What fun landmarks have you passed on your spiritual path? Are you ready to be initiated into what Swami Beyondananda calls "the ancient art of Fu-Ling?"

Fool around with new ways of doing things. Fold your hands differently. Drive (your karma) a different way to work. Brush your teeth with your other hand. And laugh at yourself along the way!

We cry because the disparity is unthinkable, and we laugh because there is no other thing we can do about it. Laughter erupts precisely as the situation becomes hopeless.

—Walter Kerr

Have you ever felt that a situation in your life was hopeless . . . but not impossible? How can you use humor to approach and embrace the unthinkable?

Keep a fortune cookie witticism in your wallet to help you gain or regain perspective when needed: "When someone says that nothing is impossible, ask him to dribble a football."

Humor is often a way of communicating that allows things to be said that couldn't be said otherwise. My hope is that if we take humor more seriously, we'll be able to enjoy it more frequently.

—*Ralph Nader*

How can you use humor today to get a message "in the back door"? How can you use humor to minimize defensiveness—in yourself and others?

Be on the lookout for fun bumper stickers that deliver serious messages. Put a fun bumper sticker on your own car.

Life does not cease to be funny when people die any more than it ceases to be serious when people laugh.

—*George Bernard Shaw*

Have you ever felt like you could die laughing?

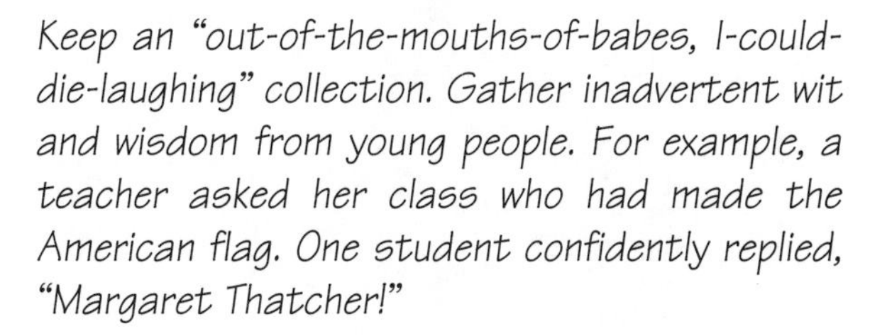

Keep an "out-of-the-mouths-of-babes, I-could-die-laughing" collection. Gather inadvertent wit and wisdom from young people. For example, a teacher asked her class who had made the American flag. One student confidently replied, "Margaret Thatcher!"

Canned laughter is the lowest form of fascism.

—Paul Krassner

Have you ever noticed that extremists don't smile?

Watch television with the sound turned down. Can the canned laughter.

Humor is the oil that keeps the engine of society from getting overheated. The best humor is based on the human comedy and has to do with ordinary situations that we're all familiar with.

—*Mary McNorton*

How does humor show up in your everyday life? How do you cool off when things get hot and heavy?

In the workplace, take over-used words and place them in a "banned words" booklet. It's a fun way to help you de-jargonize your conversations. At the same time, you can achieve total quality management of the re-engineering process.

A.S.A.P. means As Silly As Possible.

—*Alan Black*

Have you been as silly as you can be today?

Whenever you are disagreeing with someone, bet that person a nickel. It's a fun, childlike way to defuse the tension.

I have always felt sorry for people afraid of feeling, of sentimentality—who are unable to weep with their whole heart. Because those who do not know how to weep do not know how to laugh either.

—Golda Meir

Who do you miss? What do you miss? Will you allow laughter and tears to fill your cup?

Videotape or audiotape your parents and grandparents. Ask them to wax nostalgic as they share funny and touching moments from their lives.

Do not take life too seriously; you will never get out of it alive.

—Elbert Hubbard

What do you hope to get out of life? What are you willing to put into it? How can you celebrate life?

Send incongruous birthday cards to friends and family; send a card for a two-year-old to your 50-year-old friend.

Humor happens when two worlds collide. Humor is the synapse between the regular and the surprising.

—*Margie Brown*

How can you build regular surprises into your life (if that's not an oxymoron . . . or even if it is)?

Playfully warn yourself about see-food diets: the more food you see, the more you eat.

We cannot really love anybody with whom we never laugh.

—*Agnes Repplier*

What do you do to tickle your love's fancy? What feather does he or she use to tickle your funny bone?

Spend an hour at a local card shop browsing through the humorous greeting cards. If you go with someone else, pick out a card for each other.

When our knowledge coalesces with our humanity and our humor, it can add up to wisdom.

—Carol Orlock

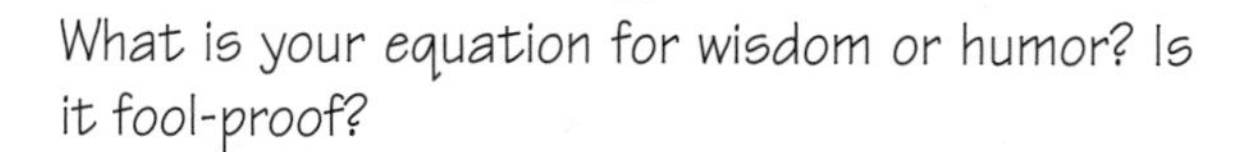

What is your equation for wisdom or humor? Is it fool-proof?

Do some mental exercise every day. Carry a list of jokes and anecdotes with you—this will jog your memory to help you access humor when you need it. Don't leave home without it.

I'm not trying to be funny all the time. I don't want to get into that lampshade mentality . . . I just travel the country and identify the absurd.

—Jay Leno

What is absurd in your life? What can you create to add to the absurdity?

Start a monthly Mismatch Day at work on which you try to wear the worst possible combos. Let's hear it (the laughter) for polka dots and plaid!

There is a very big difference between behaviors that are childish and perspectives that are childlike.

—Joel Goodman

What is the difference for you between "childish" and "childlike"? How can you use a childlike perspective today as a mature-adult coping mechanism?

Ask your children ridiculous questions to stimulate interest, thought and laughter. This helps connect their sense of wonder with their sense of humor.

Once you can laugh at your own weaknesses, you can move forward. Comedy breaks down walls. It opens up people. If you're good, you can fill up those openings with something positive. Maybe you can combat some of the ugliness in the world.

—*Goldie Hawn*

Which of your weaknesses is laughable? What random act of kindness or sense-of-humor act of beauty can you perform today?

When it's tough making a decision, reduce the pressure by saying, "If you're too open-minded, everything falls out!"

There are three things which are real: God, human folly, and laughter. The first two are beyond our comprehension, so we must do what we can with the third.

—*John F. Kennedy*

What can you do to apply laughter to human folly? What are some of your follies?

Use your word processor or desktop publishing system to make up fun plaques like, "I was so far behind I thought I was first."

Joy is not in things, it is in us.

—*Benjamin Franklin*

Where do you look for joy? Where do you find it?

Intentionally look for unintentional humor in newspaper advertisements, like the ad for an auto repair service: "Free pick-up and delivery. Try us once, and you'll never go anywhere again."

If I had no sense of humor, I should long ago have committed suicide.

—Mahatma Gandhi

What helps you keep on giving?

Make an agreement with an associate to greet each other with a joke, cartoon or anecdote every time you meet. Call each other on the phone if you haven't seen each other in a while.

Humor is like food. You have to have it every day. You have to have a sense of humor and be able to laugh at yourself.

—*Sid Caesar*

What are you thankful for when it comes to humor in your life? How can you use humor when you feel like a turkey?

Get together with friends or coworkers on a regular basis for a "turkey trot." Trot out your own laugh-at-youself stories, and give a fun prize to the person with the best "I-was-a-turkey" story. Laughing at yourself and with others can be very nourishing.

Humor is a proof of faith.

—*Charles M. Schulz*

How can you share your faith with humor today?

Keep pictures of your children on your desk along with things they've drawn for you. This will help you focus on the fun they bring to your life. You may find it helps you "draw on" your own sense of humor.

People who feel good about themselves produce good results.

—Ken Blanchard

What successes are you proud of?

Place a "message of the day" on your computer system or in your e-mail. Whenever anyone logs on, the humorous joke or quote appears; e.g., "Minds are like parachutes—they only function when open."

Instead of working for the survival of the fittest, we should be working for the survival of the wittiest; then we can all die laughing.

—Lily Tomlin

Wit's up, doc?

Whenever your coworkers have interpersonal conflicts, jokingly say, "Frogs are smart—they eat what bugs them!"

Avoid witticisms at the expense of others.

—Horace Mann

What is the cost of hurtful humor? To the receiver? To the initiator?

Humor is for giving . . . and humor is forgiving. If you suspect you have inadvertently hurt someone with humor, check it out. It will mean a lot to that person.

The human race has only one really effective weapon, and that is laughter.

—*Mark Twain*

How can you use humor to preserve yourself and your self-esteem?

Subscribe to a humor magazine like LAUGHING MATTERS *in order to give yourself an on-going injection of humor.*

ONE BRAND NEW DAY ...SIGN RIGHT HERE, PLEASE!
Tom Wilson

The time to laugh is when you don't have time to laugh.

—*Argus Poster*

What would you do differently if you only had 23 hours in a day? How about 25 hours in a day?

When you're really facing deadline pressures at work, take a one-minute humor break to brainstorm exaggerated ways you could procrastinate. It's a great way to recharge your batteries.

Lightness enlightens.

—Joel Goodman

What is one thing you do to lighten your mental load?

Make a commitment to become a "humor volunteer" in your local community. Give your time at a local hospital to set up or help out with a humor room or comedy cart for patients. Offer to help establish a kids' comedy club in a local school or youth group. Volunteer at a nursing home by reading humorous stories to the residents. Give the gift of humor . . . and you'll get a lot back in return.

Laughter is God's hand on the shoulder of a troubled world.

—Bettenell Huntzicker

Who can you reach out to today to lend a hand . . . or some heart-felt laughter?

Every Monday morning, encourage your staff or co-workers to get together for 15 minutes to share humor. This will help to "fill your tanks." You may even look forward to Mondays with a T.G.I.M. attitude!

Life is God's joke on us. It's our mission to figure out the punchline.

—*John Guarrine*

What's it all about, Alfie?

Write all your favorite punchlines and quotes in your checkbook . . . so you can laugh all the way to the bank. It also can help you laugh when trying to balance your checkbook makes you want to cry.

Laughter is the best medicine in the world.

—*Milton Berle*

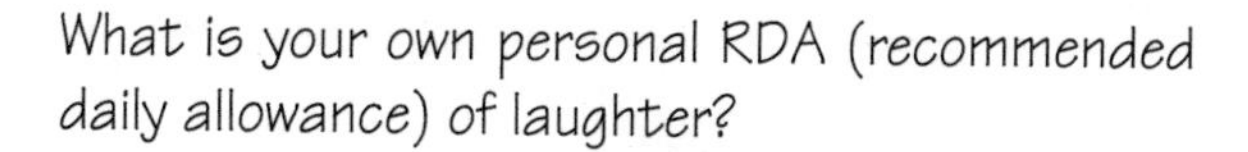

What is your own personal RDA (recommended daily allowance) of laughter?

Create your own yuck-a-day joke capsules. Type or write jokes on small sheets of paper. Roll up the papers and put them in a recycled pill bottle. Take one-a-day . . . or give one-a-day to someone who needs this kind of medicine.

You can't be sexy if you're not funny.

—Carol Burnett

Are you aware that "sense of humor" is ranked #1 in surveys of what people look for in relationships?

Just for the fun of it, write a personal ad about yourself; describe what attracts you to others, and what attracts others to you. Add a humorous touch or two.

Humor is a serious thing. I like to think of it as one of our greatest and earliest national resources which must be preserved at all costs.

 —*James Thurber*

Why should you be serious about humor? What benefits has humor provided to you—both personally and professionally?

Unlike other natural resources, the more humor you use, the more you'll have. Borrow or rent humorous videos or films from your local library or video store; show them at parties.

A person without a smiling face must not open a shop

—Chinese proverb

What can you do to give "customer service with a smile" today?

Occasionally bring an inflated plastic dinosaur to work and dress it up. With a smile in your voice, tell your customers, clients or patients, "We're a little short-staffed today."

No matter what your heartache may be, laughing helps you forget it for a few seconds.

—*Red Skelton*

What would you like to forget for at least a few seconds?

Supposedly, this is the season to be jolly. Yet, for many people, this is a time of great stress. Go and bring some good cheer, humor books and audiotapes to the homebound elderly, to a local nursing home or to your own home.

Humor is a terrific tool for explaining things, especially when what you're explaining is frightening or dull and complicated . . . All a humorist does is try to put things in perspective, and say, "Well, look, in the long run, we're all dead."

—*P.J. O'Rourke quoted in* Publishers Weekly

What is frightening, dull or complicated in your own life? How can humor help you stay alive . . . in the short fun and the long fun?

Consider the flight attendant who began his potentially dull instructions by announcing, "For those of you who have not been in a car since 1952 . . . we will now demonstrate how to use a seatbelt!" Your listeners will be chuckled in if you can use humor to deliver your message.

Comedy is a way of thinking about the world. When you stop laughing, comedy really does make you think. Comedy pulls us together and shows how human we are, and shows that we share ways of looking at the world.

—*Ejner Jensen*

How can you give the gift of humor during this season?

Give gag gifts at your annual staff holiday party. For instance, one staff gave their director the "Rear End Report." He loved it (and they still have their jobs)!

Without a sense of humor, life doesn't make much sense.

—*Bob Pearcy*

How can you make sense of the non-sense in your life?

When giving a serious presentation, insert a nonsensical statement like "My dog has dandruff" right in the middle of the sentence; then go right on talking. It captures people's attention and reduces tension, so that retention can occur.

No mind is thoroughly well organized that is deficient in a sense of humor.

—*Samuel Coleridge*

How can you organize your humor repertoire today?

Put witty sayings on your bathroom mirror as a gentle reminder of how to approach your day: "The early bird gets the worm. If you don't like worms for breakfast, get up later."

Life is not a laughing matter . . . but can you imagine having to live without laughing?

—Leonid Sukhorukov

Can you imagine what life would be like without laughter?

Make sure you read at least ten pages of a funny book every day.

Good humor is a tonic for mind and body. It is the best antidote for anxiety and depression. It is a business asset.

—*Glenville Kleiser*

How can humor serve you at work today?

Think of ways to build humor into your business signs and advertising. For instance, one man who runs an artist's supply store in Wisconsin has a sign painted on the back of his shop van: "Watch our Van Gogh!"

We joke as a refusal to ennoble suffering. When we feel oppressed and joke about it, we control the insult or punishment.

—Sarah Blacher Cohen

What feels insulting, punishing, oppressive or out of control in your life or work? How can you use levity to overcome this gravity?

Put up a funny sign in your office that states, "God made the world in only seven days, but He didn't have to do any paperwork."

The smile is the universal symbol for accepting others.

—Susan Isaacs

What can you do today to be more accepting of yourself? What can you do to be more accepting of others?

Actively look for funny people. Hang out with friends who are funny and clever. The funniest people you know just may be the ones who think you're funny!

Laughter can be more satisfying than honor; more precious than money; more heart-cleansing than prayer.

—Harriet Rochlin

What is the connection for you between laughter and prayer?

Start your day by meditating on this expression: "We need more laugh wrinkles and less worry warts."

The punchline is like the interval between thunder and enlightening.

—Joel Goodman

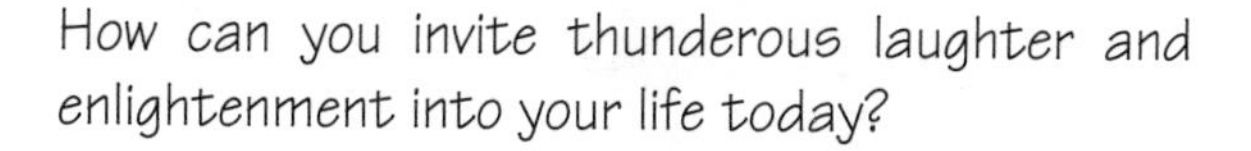

How can you invite thunderous laughter and enlightenment into your life today?

Each week, designate a person in your home or office as the recipient of a standing ovation . . . just because of who they are (not what they do).

Innocent humor (the kind that doesn't evoke laughter at another's expense) is soul-enhancing and tends to heal illness.

—*Ellen Beck*

Can you teach your sense of humor to heal? To roll over?

The next time you cross paths with people who have suffered a serious injury or bad turn of events in their lives, give them a caring look along with a simple understatement, "I bet you've had better days!" The humor of understatement can help people gain or re-gain perspective.

We are not amused.

—Queen Victoria

What is not funny to you? Are there any areas of your life where humor is not welcome?

Take a touchy area in your life . . . and add a touch of humor to it. For example, one woman is married to an electrical engineer. She surprised him one day with a sign over their bed saying "High Voltage Area!" They had a shockingly good time!

Laughter and good humor are the canaries in the mine of commerce—when the laughter dies, it's an early warning that life is ebbing from the enterprise.

—*Paul Hawken*

What are the early-warning signals that you are taking yourself too seriously?

Create your own tongue-in-cheek "sheepish skin" to hang on your office wall. For instance, one Ph.D. in nuclear physics was manager of a large plant. Unlike his colleagues who had their degrees on the wall, he had only one. It stated, "This is to certify that C. H. Millar has successfully completed third grade."

The world is a perpetual caricature of itself; at every moment it is the mockery and the contradiction of what it is pretending to be. Humor is the perception of this illusion.

—George Santayana

Which credo fits you better: "Seeing is believing" or "Believing is seeing"?

During the holidays, wrap a series of boxes—each slightly smaller than the one enclosing it, and each addressed to a different person in the family. No one knows who the final recipient will be. This element of surprise generates much magical laughter.

Shared laughter creates a bond of friendship. When people laugh together, they cease to be young and old, teacher and pupils, worker and boss. They become a single group of human beings.

—*W. Lee Grant*

How can you give the gift of laughter today to bond you with others? How can laughter create a bond with your past?

Get together with people you love and care about and share fun memories about "the good old days." For instance, one person told us, "When Mom was upset at Dad, she would pack all of us kids in the car. We would ask, 'Where are we going?' Her answer was, 'To Helen Back.' I still to this day do not know where Helen Back lives . . . but I do know that my Mom had a humor safety valve."

Humor is the essence of humanity.

—*Steve Allen*

What is the essence of you? What is at the core of your self concept? Where does your sense of humor fit in?

At work, try to achieve excellence while giving yourself permission to be human (i.e., to make mistakes). Put up a playful sign on the bulletin board, "When I am right, no one remembers. When I am wrong, no one forgets."

Laughter has no accent.

—Jim Boren

What can you do today to make the world a smaller place? How can you use humor to connect with someone who at first glance is different from you?

Register now for The HUMOR Project's annual April international conference on The Positive Power of Humor & Creativity.

The number one premise of business is that it need not be boring or dull. It ought to be fun. If it's not fun, you're wasting your life.

—*Tom Peters*

Or, as Ben & Jerry say, "If it's not fun, why do it?"

Like Ben & Jerry's®, start your own Joy Gang at work. The Joy Gang is a committee of employees whose goal is to bring more joy into the work-place. They give out Joy Grants of up to $500 to any employee who proposes an idea that will bring more joy into the corporate culture.

In the end, everything is a gag.

—*Charlie Chaplin*

How can you use humor to turn an "ending" into a "beginning"?

If you or someone you know is facing hospitalization or surgery, use humor as a mental turning point. For example, one woman sent us a note saying, "The day before my hysterectomy, I had a party for 78 people . . . a coming-out party! We had virgin Bloody Marys and deviled eggs. The laughter helped me keep perspective."

A truly happy person is one who can smile from year to year.

—O.A. Battista

What would make you truly happy today? Do it.

Recycle; go through this book again. Take in the quotes, try on the questions and try out the tips to help you smile from year to year.

Laughter loves company. . . and companies love laughter.

—*Joel Goodman*

What can you do to humorously and creatively wish Joel Goodman a happy birthday ? (Today really is his birthday!)

See the pages that follow to find out how you can get involved with Laffirmations in the future. Also, learn about other excellent humor resources available through The HUMOR Project, Inc. and Health Communications, Inc.

Is There Life After This Book?

I would love to hear from you. Please give me your feedback, as well as your feedforward.

Feedback:

What in this book has worked for you? In what ways have you adapted, modified, corrupted or applied the tips in this book? I would love to hear your success stories!

Feedforward:

Tell me your own favorite quotes about humor (including those you've cooked up yourself). Pass along your own wonders about humor—let me know what questions you have about this wonder-full subject. And let me know how you add humor to your own life and work, including your own prescriptions and humorous anecdotes.

I'll acknowledge you and your contribution in the next *Laffirmations* book.

Please send your contributions to:
Project Laffirmations
c/o The HUMOR Project, Inc.
110 Spring St.
Saratoga Springs, NY 12866

About The HUMOR Project, Inc.

Two years before Norman Cousins' best-selling book *Anatomy of an Illness As Perceived by the Patient* was published, Joel Goodman started The HUMOR Project. Since 1977, Joel's pioneering work has focused on the nature, nurture and constructive applications of humor and creativity in everyday life and work. His presentations, publications and media appearances have touched and tickled the lives of millions of people throughout the world.

The HUMOR Project offers a variety of services, resources and programs:

- The HUMOR Project sponsors the acclaimed **annual international conference** on *The Positive Power of Humor and Creativity.* Held each April, this conference fills with people from all 50 states and abroad, and has featured Jay Leno, Victor Borge, Steve Allen, Sid Caesar, the Smothers Brothers, Mark Russell, Dr. Bernie Siegel and others. This conference is a laughter- and learning-filled experience with dynamic keynote speakers and dozens of practical workshops.

- Joel also presents an **annual week-long workshop** on *The Magic of Humor and Creativity: A Personal and Professional Skillshop*, which has been filled the past 17 years.
- The HUMOR Project **Speakers Bureau** offers many excellent custom-designed workshops, staff development seminars and keynote speeches for conventions throughout the U.S. and abroad, including Japan, Taiwan, Russia, Panama, Norway, Sweden, South Africa and many other nations.
- The HUMOR Project publishes a state-of-the-art quarterly magazine, ***LAUGHING MATTERS,*** which has received rave reviews from thousands of subscribers in all 50 states and 20 other countries.
- The **HUMOResources mail-order bookstore** is the most comprehensive (and fun) collection of its kind in the world with hundreds of books, videotapes, audiocassettes, software, props and other humor/creativity resources to choose from.

To receive a **free information packet** on the positive power of humor, or for more information on arranging a program for your organization, corporation or association, contact The HUMOR Project, Inc., Dept. L, 110 Spring St., Saratoga Springs, NY 12866 (518-587-8770).

About The Author

Joel Goodman, Ed.D., founder and Director of The HUMOR Project, Inc. in Saratoga Springs, New York, is a popular speaker in the U.S. and abroad. Described as the "first full-time humor educator . . . in the vanguard of the movement to legitimize laughter," Joel has spoken to over 600,000 people at conferences and programs for corporations, hospitals, schools and associations. Author of eight books, Joel also edits *LAUGHING MATTERS* magazine. His pioneering work has been featured by thousands of TV and radio shows, newspapers and magazines, including: *The TODAY Show, CBS This Morning,* PBS, BBC, *Latenight America, All Things Considered,* the front page of *The Wall Street Journal, The New York Times, The Washington Post, USA Today, Journal of the American Medical Association, New Age Journal, Reader's Digest,* and numerous AP national features. Joel takes his work very seriously, while taking himself very lightly. In helping people to get more smileage out of their lives, he agrees with Victor Borge's notion that, "A smile is the shortest distance between two people." His own most important mentors when it comes to humor are his son, Adam, and his daughter, Alyssa.

Lessons for a Lifetime

Mentors, Masters and Mrs MacGregor
Stories of Teachers Making a Difference
Jane Bluestein, Ph.D.

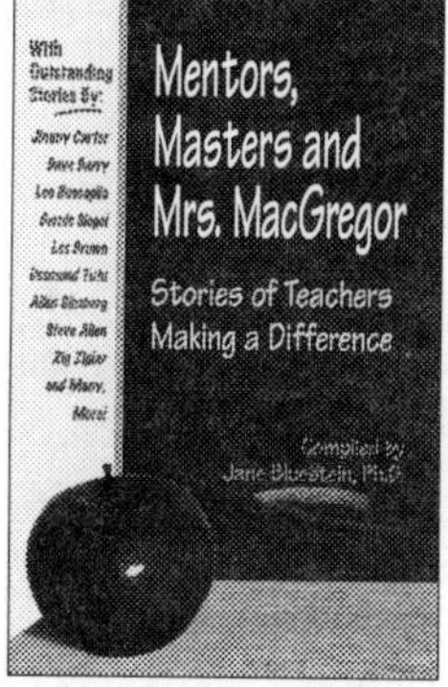

This book started with a simple question posed to thousands of people: Who is the one special teacher that made a difference in your life? Jane Bluestein, noted speaker on adult-child relationships, searched around the world for celebrities and common folks to answer this very question. *Mentors, Masters and Mrs. MacGregor* is a collection of their answers. Each story describes in beautiful detail for you the special connection that happens between a student and a real teacher. Some of the teachers are in classrooms, others are simply men and women who showed individuals how to become better people. This is a truly touching book that will appeal to the student—and the teacher—in all of us. The perfect gift for yourself or someone you love.

Code 3375: paperback $11.95
Code 3367: hard cover $22.00

Call 1-800-441-5569 for Visa or MasterCard orders. Prices do not include shipping and handling.
Your response code is HCI.

A New Story Book in the Spirit of *Chicken Soup for the Soul*

Values from the Heartland
Stories of an American Farmgirl
Bettie B. Youngs

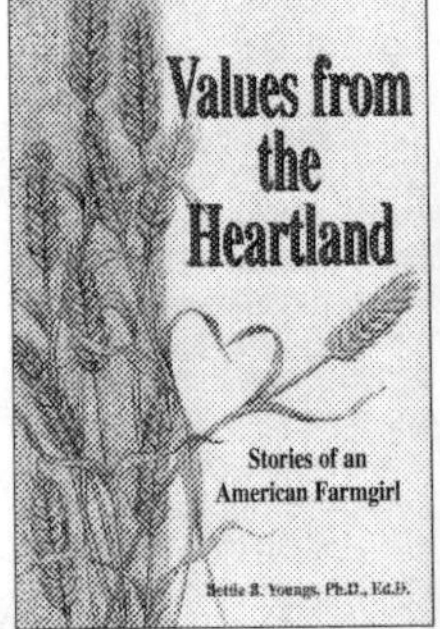

Finally, Health Communications proudly brings you a collection of Bettie Youngs' stories about growing up in America's heartland. Youngs' "Why I Chose My Father to Be My Dad" was one of the best-loved stories in *Chicken Soup for the Soul* and she has two new tales in *A 2nd Helping*; but *Values from the Heartland* is the only book that is all Bettie. These poignant tales allow you to share in the uplifting, heartwarming memories of what is enriching and lasting in life. Youngs' life in a large family was not without difficulties, yet through these value-laden stories she'll show you how hard times, when leavened with love and support, can provide strength of character, courage and leadership. A delightful book you'll read again and again.

Code 3359: paperback $11.95
Code 3340: hard cover $22.00

Call 1-800-441-5569 for Visa or MasterCard orders. Prices do not include shipping and handling.
Your response code is HCI.